"In *Kissed by a Fox*, Priscilla Stuckey explored the relationships between the human world and the natural world. Now, in *Tamed by a Bear*, she takes a radical step further as she engages a spirit animal Helper. Whether you 'believe' in the shamanic realm or are a skeptic, the insights Stuckey reaches along the way are compelling indeed. She and her Helper clearly and unequivocally convey the message that we must move from an attitude of *using* to *loving*. Best of all, *Tamed by a Bear* is an exquisitely written book. Her story—both the outer story of her search for a new place to live and the inner one of her journey to come home to herself—is told in a powerful narrative you won't soon forget."

—Linda Tate, author of *Power in the Blood: A Family Narrative*

"What affinities does *Tamed by a Bear* have with other works of spiritual seeking and connection? Purge the hallucinogens from Carlos Castaneda's *The Teachings of Don Juan*, and you might approximate it. Or perhaps it comes close to a nonfiction version of Daniel Quinn's *Ishmael*, with a playful bear as a guide, not a Socratic gorilla, of course. In the end, *Tamed by a Bear* may be in a category all its own, an account both personal and heartfelt about the author's journey to listen more fully to the voice within and the world without, even when that means—especially when that means—letting go of the known for uncharted territory."

—Gavin Van Horn, Center for Humans and Nature and coeditor of *City Creatures*

"An openhearted, playful account of learning to listen to the wisdom of interconnection."

—Elizabeth Enslin, author of *While the Gods Were Sleeping: A Journey Through Love and Rebellion in Nepal*

"Priscilla Stuckey shines a brilliant light on the relationship we long to cultivate with the deepest wellsprings of our wisdom and love. With Bear, her animal Helper, she shares her Journey to a life of communion between spirit and our physical nature. This is a groundbreaking book, written with extraordinary clarity, beauty, and radical honesty."

—Gail D. Storey, author of *I Promise Not to Suffer: A Fool for Love Hikes the Pacific Crest Trail*, winner of the National Outdoor Book Award

"After publishing her first book, Priscilla Stuckey feels surprisingly lost. In an effort to find her path, she embarks with some skepticism on a journey, a shamanic journey, and takes us with her every step of the way. Written with grace and simplicity—and luminous descriptions of nature—each of the 67 short chapters embodies a teaching. As Priscilla finds her path unfolding, one step at a time, we too are shown how to listen deeply and find more acceptance and joy . . . and a deeper relationship with all of life. Like Bear, this book is warm, engaging, and wise. A journey worth taking."

—Rivvy Neshama, author of award-winning *Recipes for a Sacred Life: True Stories and a Few Miracles*

"*Tamed by a Bear* is a wonderful surprise! Not only will this book change the way you see the world, it will change your life. With artistry, mastery, and patience, Priscilla Stuckey, along with the help of Bear, breaks through the barriers of the skeptical mind and invites the reader to share in the intimate dialogue between a human and their unseen Helper."

—Betsy Perluss, PhD, Wilderness Guide, School of Lost Borders

"In Priscilla Stuckey's latest book, we are warmly encouraged to enjoy rearranging our lives to honor our relations in the larger-than-human world. This is not another DIY shamanism or self-help manual. It is an intimate reflection on listening, on trusting our senses, on being in the world. It is about rooting ourselves in concern for well-being for everyone we know and encounter, including ourselves."

—Graham Harvey, Open University, UK, author of *Animism: Respecting the Living World* and editor of *Shamanism: A Reader*

"In *Tamed by a Bear*, Priscilla Stuckey chronicles her journey into the heart of this numinous living world, guided by a stunningly wise and delightfully down-to-earth bear spirit. This story is an extraordinary and courageous gift, full of wisdom riding on the shoulders of joy."

—Susan J. Tweit, author of *Walking Nature Home: A Life's Journey*

"Dialogue is a staple format in mystical writings, and for good reason. Whether we're eavesdropping on Arjuna and Krishna in the *Bhagavad Gita*, or the pilgrim and his *staretz* in *Way of a Pilgrim*, the conversations can start to feel personal, because in a very real sense, Arjuna is a stand-in for you and me; his questions are uncannily close to the ones we ourselves would raise if we could. Taking up a shamanic practice brought Priscilla Stuckey to the infinitely wise and tender teacher she calls, simply, 'Bear.' Their conversations, recorded in Stuckey's lovely new book, demonstrate the age-old power of the mystical dialogue itself—to draw us in and make us feel that Bear is *our* teacher too—our *staretz*, our Krishna."

—Carol Lee Flinders, author of *Enduring Grace: Living Portraits of Seven Women Mystics*

"*Tamed by a Bear* is an adventure story, about an inner journey available to us all. Author Priscilla Stuckey shares with honesty and insight her relationship with Bear, the spirit guide and helper who appears in her inner world to teach her about the things we need to know most: joy, relationship, receiving help, and welcoming the adventure or everyday life. Her stories delight and challenge us to consider the inter-beingness of reality and the wealth of support and guidance that is available to us all. It lifted me, reminded me of what I thought I could never forget. And I am grateful."

—Oriah "Mountain Dreamer" House, author of *The Invitation*

"Every page of this book sparkles with wise, clear, profoundly important insight that will resonate with anyone seeking reconciliation and communion with the Earth community. This is spiritual wisdom earned by quieting enough to receive guidance from within and without. In a time when technological clamor threatens to overwhelm our lives and devastate the planet, Priscilla Stuckey offers a simple, but not easy, path forward through the noise. This is essential reading for any spiritual or ecological warrior."

—Elizabeth Allison, PhD, Founder and Chair of the
Ecology, Spirituality, and Religion graduate program at
the California Institute of Integral Studies

"With wisdom and a sweet tempo, Priscilla shares her process of trust and receiving through a beautifully envisaged and shaped journey."

—Joanie Clingan, Prescott College, Faculty Emeritus in Sustainability
Education and Arts & Humanities

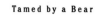

Tamed by a Bear

Tamed by a Bear

COMING HOME TO NATURE-SPIRIT-SELF

· · · · ·

Priscilla Stuckey

COUNTERPOINT
BERKELEY, CALIFORNIA

Tamed by a Bear
Coming Home to Nature-Spirit-Self

Copyright © 2017 by Priscilla Stuckey
First Counterpoint hardcover edition: July 2017

ISBN: 978-1-61902-955-2

The Library of Congress Cataloging-in-Publication Data is available.

Jacket designed by Debbie Berne
Book designed by Domini Dragoone

COUNTERPOINT
2560 Ninth Street, Suite 318
Berkeley, CA 94710
www.counterpointpress.com

Printed in the United States of America
Distributed by Publishers Group West

10 9 8 7 6 5 4 3 2 1

Devise a way
That the eye not shut
And yet the world vanish

Since drowning is inevitable
Never trust the boat
But do
Trust the river.

—Kailash Vajpeyi
Trans. from the Hindi by Ananya Vajpeyi

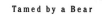

Tamed by a Bear

1

Sparkling waves rolled up the gentle slope and melted away beneath an undulating line of bubbly sand. One wave. Then another. Two more. Another.

I tried to enjoy their steady calm. It was eighty degrees in Santa Monica on a cloudless day in February. The breeze was slight, just right. In the distance surfers raced to catch each fresh inviting swell. Two dolphins pursued a small motorboat, leaping in unison, gliding below, then leaping again. I sat in the sand with my jeans and sleeves rolled up to bare sun-starved winter skin to this deliciously warm air. Swimsuits of every shape and size paraded past, legs and arms and bellies swaying between me and the blue waves.

I should have been happy. I was living the last, and most elusive, of my big dreams. Five months earlier my first book had been published—a memoir showing my deepening connection with nature—and I was having the time of my life doing readings in cities across the country and crashing for the night in the homes of friends. Here in Los Angeles, a last-minute scramble for a place to stay had landed me in a stately Mediterranean house of cool wooden floors and smooth white archways, its windows thrown open to mourning doves cooing at dawn among the eaves and palm trees waving high over birds-of-paradise in the garden below. And now—a perfect day with a perfectly hot sun, made for lolling on the beach.

The trouble was, I couldn't enjoy it. Even worse, I didn't exactly know why. It wasn't the readings. Last night's bookstore event had gone well as usual, a magic taking hold as people listened. Tomorrow I would read at a hip new literary series in a Hollywood bar, a once-a-month soiree where emerging writers tried out edgy or heartwarming lines in front of an enthusiastic crowd. No, the readings felt wonderful. Then what was it?

There was, of course, the realization I'd had that morning. Lying in bed, with doves murmuring inches from the window, I'd felt a weight descend: trips like this just weren't worth it—certainly not in terms of book sales, and maybe not by any kind of reckoning. I was late to this truth; others had been saying it for years.

But did that really explain it—this feeling of something nibbling away at my middle, and going on nibbling, oblivious to my squirming? It was a gnawing that left me restless, edgy, irritable—what writers of an earlier age called the fantods, though I didn't know this word at the time. I just knew something was out of place, not quite adding up. I felt awful. And I hated it.

From my spot on the sun-drenched sand, I called a friend who used to live in LA. We'd walked this beach together many times, and I wanted her to know I was thinking of her, and of all those blustery days we'd watched the sea roll gray and green under a dense and foggy sky.

"You wouldn't believe how gorgeous it is today!" I said. "Wish you were here." Then I told her about the edgy feeling eating away at my middle, the sense that all was not well.

"It sounds like at this point you were expecting something more," she said quietly.

I hung up the phone feeling even more discontent.

2

Back home in Boulder, I repacked myself into layers of long johns and turtlenecks and braced for March snows. Nestled against the eastern face of the Rockies, Boulder gets its biggest dumps of snow in March and April, which lends some credence to the saying that snow in Boulder never lasts. If a blizzard arrives in December—but it usually doesn't—the snow will indeed stick to sidewalks and driveways, slicking them with black ice for the rest of the winter. I've taken more than one tumble on that invisible glaze. But if snow arrives in March and April—and it often does, a foot-deep layer of wet heavy white accumulating in an afternoon or a night—the warming sun of spring will melt it to nothing in a day or so. Native plants along the Front Range have evolved great tricks for outwitting the spring blizzards. My favorite, the pasqueflower, grows a layer of furry hairs on the outside of its stem and three huge lavender petals to keep the snow a millimeter or two away from delicate flesh.

But after six years in Boulder, I wasn't yet native, and I dreaded the spring snows.

Plus there were those sliding book stats. Say what people would about book tours, they did keep the Amazon numbers in a more rarefied range. Every book trip, every public talk bumped the sales number up, where it would hover for a few days as if trying to make up its mind. Such a fragile thing, that graph of rising numbers, shooting upward like a fledging bird on delicate wings, suddenly freed to the sky, fluttering, joyous! My heart would stop. Maybe this time momentum would catch the bird and hold it aloft. But so far it hadn't happened. The line would turn downward again, and with it my heart.

I knew full well that watching numbers was futile. Knowing it only made the gnawing inside grow sharper, more determined.

And what about the next stage of my life? I'd had the feeling that this book would lead somewhere new—exactly where, I had no idea, but it would likely be a place to settle in and make a contribution. My friend had been right; I was expecting something more to open up. And I was eager for that next assignment. In each new city I checked out nature centers and environmental departments in universities and amount of winter sunshine. Tim was self-employed too, so we could move wherever we wanted. We could turn on a dime.

But the days, and then weeks and months, were creeping by with no appealing prospects on the horizon. One tenure-track position in religious studies opened up in a city known for its sunshine. The job description sounded as if it had been written for me, which is saying something, considering my specialty in the field is rather new and vanishingly small. I thought about it; I gave a lecture at that university. But did I really want academic work anyway—another decade or two of begging students to focus their research questions and reformat their reference lists? In the end I didn't even apply.

I kept thinking about the book readings—how an audience might begin as disparate, mildly curious individuals but almost always ended as something else, something more like a community. How, as listeners opened to a story, their eyes wide as children's, a silence would steal across the room and settle quietly like a blanket around their shoulders. How my own heart softened and opened each time I watched it happen. How each reading, each talk, reminded me that all of us—animals, trees, rocks, galaxies—are in it together on this journey. Each reading took me to that still and loving center where we're all connected and we're all whole. I wanted more of *that*.

So I kept on setting dates for book events, sending out bios and photos for publicity, making travel plans, and calling faraway friends. And kept on being dogged by the sinking realization that not only did we not have the money to support this habit—and it was using a frightful amount of energy, both mine and the Earth's—but also that in the long run it would never, ever be worth it.

3

As February slid into March and snow glistened outside the window, my inner crisis deepened. I felt stymied, all forward motion grinding to a halt. I might have been seventeen again, waiting for my real life to begin. Almost forty years later, with all those decades of living behind me, how could I possibly be staring again at the same impasse?

"I don't know where I belong!" I wailed to Tim, my longtime love. The book had gathered up seemingly unrelated pieces of experience and fitted them into one place. Writing it had required all of me—a demand that was both joyous and satisfying to fulfill. At last I'd found my real work! And now I wanted more of it. Or at least more of what "being a writer" had to give. The fact that most of the time I didn't actually feel like writing seemed beside the point; I barely registered it.

More troubling by far was what the plunging book numbers seemed to suggest about the future. What if the "something more" I wanted from writing never did materialize? What did that say about all the beliefs I held dear—of the Universe as a friendly, welcoming place, ready to make room for each person's gifts? Ready to make room—more to the point—for mine?

A chasm was opening in front of me.

I sat around the house feeling unglued. Reading, my go-to solace, held no pleasure. For the first time in decades I found it difficult to concentrate on a book. I got hooked on phone games instead, losing hours at a time to Solitaire or Words with Friends. Desperate to fill more time, I downloaded Angry Birds and spent several days nonstop lobbing tiny bird bombs into impenetrable fortresses.

Finally I had to agree with the small part of me that whispered, "This is madness." With Tim as my witness—so I'd be less tempted to change my mind—I deleted the app and all its data from my phone.

And then, in mid-March, I started my next four sessions with the shaman.

4

Chris was a woman of near sixty, born and raised in the Midwest, who in her early forties, with two decades of a business career behind her, had been called to work with what she called Spirit Helpers. Because the friend who had recommended Chris to me was a down-to-earth and gutsy woman, and especially because this same friend had been a Rhodes Scholar, I figured Chris couldn't be too much of a slouch.

On the phone with Chris for the first time, months before, I'd heard a calm and thoughtful voice, warm and reassuring but no-nonsense. At the time I'd just finished writing the book, and I needed clarity about what was to happen next—all the questions I'd let slide during the writing process. Plus I was dreading the upcoming months of waiting until the book would finally emerge. An edge had crept into my voice—impatient, self-justifying; I can hear it now in the recordings of those sessions, though at the time I was anything but aware of it.

Chris practiced a straightforward kind of conversation with spirit. She said that each person is watched over by their own Spirit Helper, often an animal or other being, who loves and supports a person throughout their life and who provides a face—a point of contact, a relationship—for connecting with spirit. Chris called Helpers "ambassadors of the Living Spirit"; they are always ready to share advice and wisdom from a source beyond human knowing if only a person gets up the courage to ask for it. Chris, who had been tuning her ear to Helpers for twenty years, was practiced in hearing each person's Helper, and on the phone she acted as a translator, listening quietly for a few moments and then passing along what she'd heard.

From the start, more than a year earlier, I had loved those phone sessions. I took to them like a duckling to water, wading onto the surface and bobbing happily. In each session I felt deeply listened to, the desires of my heart known and addressed, often without my having to articulate them. Every suggestion for the next steps to take arrived in down-to-earth language, with words that often carried the ring of my own vocabulary. Each session gave me the sense that help is available for this murky thing called life. I felt deeply nourished.

My Helper, whom Chris identified as Bear, got down to business right away. I was given affirmation for the path I was taking as well as suggestions for how to walk in it more effectively. Bear did hint ever so gently that when it came to listening to spirit I had a great deal more to learn—that even though I'd just written a whole book about spirit in nature, I had barely scratched the surface. "If one believes that help from a source outside human knowing is not possible, it will be a self-fulfilling prophecy," Bear said one day, an impersonal generality that gives me a chuckle because now I can hear the clue that Bear was offering—politely, obliquely—about *my* beliefs and *my* next step. But at the time I was tone-deaf to his nuances.

I did have to agree with Bear's point, however. For no matter how much my heart was feasting on the sessions, my mind was drumming it in to me, with the *rat-a-tat* of a woodpecker at a tree, that this Helper business was likely all a crock. Communicating directly with anything unseen is not possible, it said, and to think otherwise suggests some serious misperceptions of reality.

It's not that I didn't believe that something greater than human wisdom exists. I liked to hint now and then, as people do, about "the Universe," a word satisfyingly vague, not like *God* or *spirit* or any of the old words belonging to religions we had left behind or now regarded—often for good reason—with mistrust.

But to speak directly with that Universe? Let alone in a conversational, friendly way? Not possible. What happened in those sessions offended every rational notion I held dear.

For one thing, there was that word *shamanism*. It was the term Chris used to describe her path, but it made me wince. I was aware how contentious it is, how it triggers pain for every Native person I have ever met or whose writings I have read. *Shaman* is a Tungus word—from the northern Indigenous peoples of Siberia—to name the person who keeps the human community safe and healthy by communicating with all those who are not human, such as the animals or the land or the deceased. Decades ago, white anthropologists took the word and applied it to any Indigenous nature-based healer and spirit worker they found anywhere in the world. So when a white person calls themselves a shaman, using that Indigenous term, what Indians usually hear is that the white person is trying to steal or at least copy Indigenous wisdom, Indigenous sacred traditions, Indigenous ways. It's the whole of colonialism summed up in a single word.

"Why wouldn't people just call themselves healers? Or ministers? Or soul-doctors—something like that?" an Indian friend of mine asked, staring sharply at me, when I brought it up with her. "Why do you have to use an Indigenous word?" It was a good question.

Then there was that translating business. Chris said she heard a spirit-being talking with her, giving her things to say, but how did she know it wasn't her own voice? I didn't for a moment think she was *trying* to make it up—she had far too much integrity for that—but neither did I think it was possible to hear across the great divide between the visible and the invisible, at least not without the message getting considerably skewed by the messenger. Maybe spirit does flow like pure water, but doesn't every pitcher change the water's shape? A person's own physiology, their personality, their social context, their history—it all bends what they hear, doesn't it?

Not to mention how easy it is to fool ourselves. Perception is such a shifty character! A shape-shifting octopus, now rough-skinned and blotchy on the mottled reef, now lifting off in a burst of inky darkness and smooth writhing limbs. We thought we knew what we were seeing, but the reality wasn't what we saw. I'd long ago heard the parable of the snake from centuries-old Vedanta. A man walking along a road at dusk sees a snake and runs in great fear. But the next day at noon, coming to the same point in the road, he sees it was not a snake at all but only a coil of rope. Snake or rope? It can be devilishly hard to tell. "Now we see through a glass, darkly," wrote the apostle Paul to the ancient Corinthians, which pretty much summed up my own view on the matter. I may have yearned for reality to be different, but the truth was—as my industrious woodpecker of a mind never ceased to remind me—that knowledge beyond the world of the five senses is impossible, and even here in this tactile world so much depends on your perspective, your point of view.

And then there was the biggest bugaboo of all: How could I trust anyone who claimed to speak words from God? After decades of studying religion, I was aware that recorded history, at least in the parts of the world I knew best, might well be written as a single ginormous argument between people on one side—individuals, groups, nations—saying, "God told us this!" and on the other side, "No! God told us *that!*" All the murder, rape, and pillage committed in the name of the divine, the forced conversions and slavery imposed through supposedly divine orders—it all took place side by side with kindness to strangers, sharing with the poor, and humbleness of heart, virtues also supposedly recommended by that same divine. So how could I possibly believe anyone's claims to hear the "real" God? Like most modern people, I was sensitive to any whiff of "God said this," and I regarded all such claims with a big dose of skepticism. To be perfectly honest, I discounted them all. Every last one. New Agers who claimed to hear Spirit Guides or Helpers were, to my mind, even less trustworthy. For no person, as far as I knew, could really hear God. There was no Extendable Ear reaching to heaven.

All of which left me living a huge contradiction, as even I had to admit. During book readings I was talking with audiences about how wonderful life could become if only we listened to animals, trees, and Earth more deeply, and in between trips I would sign up for more sessions of listening, through Chris, to my animal Spirit Helper. Yet, though Bear said during those sessions that I had a facility for hearing the Helpers, and though Bear recommended that I allow my connection with spirit to deepen and flourish, for without that connection a person walks crooked through life—a hitch in their step—and though Bear said plainly that one of my contributions in life would have to do with listening to wisdom from another realm and offering it to others, I didn't have confidence in any of what I heard. I couldn't bring myself to believe it was real.

Though I was enjoying the sessions with Chris immensely, I was having a hard time taking them at all seriously.

5

On the phone with Chris in mid-March I tried to put my dilemma into words—loss of direction, too much snow—but before I could get very far, she suggested a shift. Up to this point in the sessions Chris had acted as translator and interpreter, and I would listen while she passed along what she received from Bear. Today, instead, she would stand by, taking notes, while I listened directly to Bear. She called it "going on a Journey" with one's Helper. "Want to give it a try?" she asked.

I closed my eyes and immediately sensed a bear—good-humored and warmhearted—rubbing paws together gleefully and chuckling at me. The sensation was so unexpected, and so welcoming, that I decided to play along. What harm could come of seeing where this fantasy led? There was a sense of sympathy too, as if this bear, though amused at the situation, was also commiserating in a kindly way.

I spoke aloud what I was sensing from Bear so that Chris could hear. Why did it feel so strange to voice what I was experiencing? It took me a moment to remember that though I had grown up in a praying family and a praying church, I'd always shrunk from speaking prayers aloud. This Journey was the closest thing to prayer I had experienced in years, and narrating it aloud made my skin crawl with self-consciousness.

I swallowed hard and kept going. Some images appeared of a locomotive rolling through lush green land—images that Chris and I spent a few moments looking at together, noting but not analyzing. Then a picture of a wide-open blue sky with the thought, "It's okay right now not to read books; just stare into space if you like." A feeling that all would be well if I continued to let my mind empty and allowed it to stay that way "because that's one route to appreciating spaciousness." Not to worry about how I would make a living in the future; it would not be a problem. And then a strong sense of something like this: that the end of the story had not been written yet, and I shouldn't jump to conclusions. That if I could calm my impatience, the story would go a lot smoother.

Soon the session was over.

6

There is a danger in describing how this path unfolded for me. One person's experience recorded in detail can leave the impression that there is a pattern, a usual way for things to happen. Nothing could be further from the truth. One person might slip easily into meditative Journeys while another spends years practicing, yet each is walking in the center of their own road, discovering what is theirs alone to discover. The Universe helps people toward clarity through many different means. There is no formula, no right way. Each traveler is held by the same loving hands, guided by the best wisdom toward their own particular destination. For some travelers the path may include meditative or shamanic Journeys; for others it may not.

In my case, though I had an aptitude for Journeys, I stumbled on this speaking-aloud business. I could understand what Chris meant when she said that it tended to help the mind stay focused on what was happening in the Journey. I could even appreciate that recording a Journey, as she recommended, would help jog the memory later about its nuances. But speaking aloud? It just felt strange.

Nevertheless, two days later when for the first time in my life I fumbled on my own toward that inner connection with Bear, I did it with cell phone in hand, narrating what I experienced into a phone app—modern technology applied to an old, old kind of meditation.

Just after six that morning I climbed out of bed and wrapped myself in a blanket to ward off the night's chill. The world was dark and still. Tim wouldn't be up for a while yet, and Bodhi, our blue heeler mix, was still curled up in his favorite spot on the sofa. I turned on the phone recorder and tried to bring my mind into a still center.

Immediately images of the locomotive returned. *Click-e-ta, click-e-ta, click-e-ta.* A train moving along the tracks, steady, humming. I described what I saw and heard into the phone. There was a feeling of confidence in the train's momentum, as if I were suddenly a passenger on that train, traveling swiftly forward. How I wished for such a feeling in real life! What would it take for me to travel that smoothly? Then a thought, like a very gentle voice in my ear. I spoke it into the phone: "Notice how putting yourself there imaginatively already makes you feel more put together. More hearty. More here." It was true; the sturdy rhythm beneath my imaginary feet was helping my physical voice grow a little stronger. "Try starting here. Every day," the gentle presence suggested.

Just then, more than three miles from our house, a train approaching town laid on its horn. Though all our windows were shut tight against the wintry dawn, the sound of the horn slipped inside the house and into my quiet time with Bear. The phone mic even picked it up. "Is there more about being on a train?" I asked, wanting to understand the image more fully.

The train blared again. *Whooooo. Whoooo-hoooo.*

I waited for more insight. Then waited a little more. I had no idea where to go from here. Finally it dawned on me: this not-knowing point in the conversation was exactly how I felt in outer life. As soon as I spoke that thought, a new suggestion arose: that just as I was learning to trust that some little piece of a picture would show up in the Journey, this would be good to practice in outer life as well.

The train bellowed once, then again. A double exclamation point.

As the train receded and finally grew silent, different images appeared. I caught a glimpse of jigsaw pieces—familiar from years I'd spent putting puzzles together in childhood. What was it about puzzle pieces? Bear responded immediately: "They come in from different corners. You sometimes have to search a while for the right one, the one that fits. But when it fits, it *really* fits. There's no making it fit. It's *made* to fit."

That's when I lost it, sobbing quietly into the phone. How fervently I longed for such a fit, how afraid I'd become that it would never be possible!

Bear's thoughts continued. "There will be no sense of having to trim the corners. It is a smooth and perfect fit because it was cut that way." And then a piece of advice: "Reside in the feeling that you know so well from hundreds of hours of putting puzzles together—a piece slipping into place with the ease of water flowing downhill. Look for *that*." Bear explained: "Don't get sidetracked by the pieces that almost fit. Look instead for the one that slides rightfully into place. You will know it when you feel it."

My voice was growing lighter, almost playful, with each passing minute. Finally I glimpsed an image of a large puzzle completely put together and heard the Helper say, "Take comfort from knowing that this piece fits into a larger picture. There is an intention behind it."

This was followed by a feeling of completion, except for one parting image, a bear standing up with one forearm placed quietly across the heart: a greeting, a pledge. "Remember the heart connection. Come here often."

I thanked Bear, turned off the recorder, and glanced at the clock. In only twenty minutes my life had changed.

Something big had just happened, though I couldn't grasp exactly what. This much I knew: I'd experienced an unseen partner in this conversation. All those years I'd spent praying as a young person, sending out pleas to a huge and empty sky, but now, at last, I had heard someone speaking back. The words felt familiar yet unfamiliar as well. They were not mine, yet I felt their truthfulness in my body, in my heart. I heard their message in the silence of my mind and then heard it punctuated in the "real" world. In a twist I couldn't have engineered, a train sounded its horn across town at the very moment I was experiencing the sensation of being a railway passenger.

Something more than I could fathom or control was going on here.

7

After that morning I engaged in regular Journey sessions, curling up with my phone almost every day in a private spot in the house and listening quietly for what might come. I still faltered, my voice unsteady, my heart not quite daring to believe. Yet from each session I gained a feeling that I was not alone on this journey of life, that someone unseen had my back. In each session my question of the day would be addressed, and always there would come a sense of completion, a feeling that "we're over for today," whether or not I was ready for the time to end. With each session my sense of amazement grew. This Journey business—it wasn't a one-time deal.

As I began to trust the conversations, my feeling of disorientation deepened. Outwardly I kept doing the work of promoting a book—reaching out to people in emails, sending out book copies for reviews—but inside I was being tugged somewhere else, somewhere away from books, away from the writer identity that just a few weeks ago I'd been so sure I wanted. I felt the pull of another world. I tired easily, my eyes glazing over and my brain switching off sooner than expected. If reading a book had turned suddenly difficult during the preceding weeks of crisis, now it became impossible. I lost all mental focus. I had zero interest in other people's words.

Grasping for something to do, I hauled old jigsaw puzzles out from storage, hoping to feel under my fingers that sense of easy fit. For most of a week Tim and I hunkered together over the dining room table, fitting puzzle pieces into place.

During this time Bear showed me a close-up image of feet planted on a path. Next to this path was another one aimed in a slightly different direction so that by the time they reached the horizon, the two paths had grown very far apart. As I watched, first one foot and then the other lifted off the path it was on and picked its way sideways onto the other. "Pay attention to how the feet are planted," Bear advised. "It is not a trivial matter to step crosswise from one path to another."

It was true; my body was beginning to feel like putty, as if I'd had a little too much to drink and now was having to concentrate very hard to cross a room without weaving. The ground itself seemed less solid, threatening to heave upward at the lightest footfall. I stepped gingerly through each day and tried to avoid driving.

Some days I felt raw, my heart sliced open. Simple things seemed unbearably sweet. When, about a week after my first Journey with Bear, I visited a tiny school up in the mountains to speak with young children about connecting with nature, my eyes glistened the entire time. The stories the children told about their dog or their cat or the love they felt for a fox they'd glimpsed in the woods near their house or the kindness they'd shown a spider; how they knew, just knew, at six or seven or eight years old, exactly how to let other beings touch their hearts; how they savored this love, and how it lit their wide-open, sincere faces—I could barely make it through the hour for the sweetness.

Many days I felt murky, more confused than it seemed possible. One morning Bear drew my attention to the clay pots resting in the bay window—their pleasing lines, their intriguing colors. I'd fashioned them during fifteen years of taking ceramics classes at local studios. The pots looked clear and peaceful, but I knew that the hours spent laboring over them in the studio had not felt that way. Especially when I worked on the wheel, there seemed to be no connection at all between how I felt on the inside and what my hands turned out. After a day that radiated with clarity, I might arrive at the studio and not be able to center the clay at all. The opposite was just as true: I might sit down one evening at the wheel feeling completely off balance, only to witness the clay growing as if by itself into graceful miracles under my hands. These pots on the windowsill were some of my largest and most graceful, and I remembered they had arrived in this way as gifts.

"Such things of beauty that can come out of murkiness," Bear observed. Did I see a twitch of a smile?

"Okay, I think I got that!" I said, laughing.

"Good work is a gift," Bear went on. "It doesn't depend on the maker's state of mind." Matter of fact, he said, when a person creates something while experiencing that sense of internal clarity, they are tempted to take full credit for the result. They think they can manage the output. "Many people do manage the product in that way," he added. "And it's much harder to reach the deeper gift when you go that route."

He said in a reassuring tone, "One doesn't have to feel clear to be of great value and make a great contribution. One only needs to be malleable."

8

The ground of Tim's and my lives was shifting in other ways as well. The friends who had rented us their home while they explored retiring abroad decided to stay in England and sell their Boulder property. The grip of the calendar tightened when I found buyers for the house—a couple down the street whom I'd met during early morning swims in the neighborhood pool. Late in the previous fall they'd looked at the house, loved it, and put in an offer. Since January, two months earlier, the house we were living in had been under contract. Though the final sale depended on the buyers selling their own house, sometime this year we would have to move. I began keeping my eyes open for another place to live.

Two weeks after my first meditative Journey, Bear introduced a new theme. "Keep looking forward to good things," Bear said. "When one senses that change is on the way, it can be easy to slip into dreading it, being frightened of it. Keep anticipating it with great enjoyment." Along with the words came an image of a bear standing up and shaking off, getting ready to go. My homework, Bear said, would be to keep steadying my mind in what he called "ebullient good enjoyment." I smiled; the words—and the sentiment—were so unlike me.

"This robust good enjoyment provides energy," Bear continued. "It also gives you a solid platform on which to move—the fuel as well as the foundation." Bear said enjoyment was like a buffer, helping to strengthen a person so that one has the stamina for handling the more challenging assignments in life.

"How can I contact this enjoyment?" I asked.

No need to work for it, he said. "Just crack the door, and it's there. It doesn't take much encouragement. Watch Bodhi. Or spend time with a child. Or just look out the window." This thought was accompanied by a picture of double doors in a floor, like a trapdoor or a chute leading downward. As soon as the doors cracked open, I spotted a cheery warm light down below. The idea, apparently, was just to drop into the warm light, into enjoying life.

"Just slide down the chute of enjoyment!" Bear said, cracking up. He was nearly beside himself with merriment.

It was April Fool's Day.

9

As I listened to Bear's voice, my own voice began to shift—growing lighter during each session, a shift plainly audible over the course of each recording. Many mornings I woke up too early, at three or four, feeling jangled, trying hard to restore some sense of peace and fall asleep again. Sometimes it worked, but often it didn't, leaving my voice at the start of a Journey later that morning still sounding heavy, questing. Yet without fail, after only ten or twenty minutes of chatting with Bear I would lighten up, my voice easier, more amused. Bear, I discovered, was nudging me toward a more cheerful frame of mind.

It took only a few weeks for Tim to start commenting on the change. "You seem happier," he said. He was right. Though the prospect of moving was staring us in the face, and though Tim was still deep in the throes of career change and I was bringing in practically no money so that family finances looked worse than terrible, and though I had no idea where this Journey practice was heading and no clue how I might be able to earn a living—or when—my outlook was indeed becoming more cheerful. How could it not? I was hanging out with a perpetually cheerful Bear who seemed to think that the purpose of life is to enjoy it. Under Bear's influence, I was beginning to enjoy it more too.

Buoyed by the changes I could feel happening within, I looked forward to my almost-daily time with Bear. That sense of communion, that feeling of Bear like a warm cloak around my shoulders— every time I returned to it helped me nestle a little more firmly within its sanctuary.

However, just because I was receiving a sense of warm support from communing with Bear, a feeling that I was hearing and being heard, doesn't mean that the Journeys flowed naturally from the start. Much of the time in those early weeks I felt that I was taking lessons in a foreign language, trying to shape my mouth around an awkward "Hello! . . . How . . . er . . . are . . . you?"

One day I noticed that a Journey flowed more easily if I kept my attention a little lighter, like floating across the top of a river's currents instead of staring hard into the water, studying each eddy, trying to figure out where to navigate next. The habit of watching the river a little too closely only yielded a ponderous, slow conversation. Slipping into that heavy mental focus seemed to be one of the ways in which, as Chris liked to say, "we get our own fingers in the mix." The mind begins to think it has to work hard, and instantly the magic is gone; one no longer feels buoyed up by friendly forces. If I started to work too hard, it was likely a signal that my own mind, not my Helper, had begun to direct the flow. Giving my Helper a freer rein meant bringing a lighthearted, even playful, spirit to the process—a spirit of trust, a spirit of fun. Journeys were meant to be enjoyable, to feed the soul.

But at the same time, skimming across the surface of a river of pretty thoughts or concepts was not flowing with the Helper either.

It was a mind sailing away on a frothy feeling and losing all connection to the heart. I had to stay simpler than that.

"No fancy thinking," Bear said. "Following one of those tempting, beautiful trails can get in the way of simplicity." The best thing to do, if I felt myself about to spin away on a gorgeous thought, was to pause and breathe, to come back to the body, back to the heart. To focus again on my Helper. "It doesn't take fancy mental dance moves," Bear said. "More simple, more love. Which is also more open."

That's why, Bear explained, coming back to the body is always a good thing to do. "Compassion for the body and for the material world is a sure foundation," he said. Was I trying to ignore the body, or was I opening fully, with love, to all its physical weaknesses? "Accepting what is in each moment—that is the greatest simplicity," Bear said. "It's a good way to check," he added, "that one is seeing clearly."

Trying to master the grammar of this new language, hoping to become fluent, I practiced keeping my attention focused yet open and light, in that Goldilocks place of "just right."

10

Bear, I soon discovered, was a fan of being oneself, whoever that self happened to be. "One needs to live from that foundation of knowing the beauty of spirit within oneself," Bear said one day in early April. To find one's place in the world, he recommended settling deeper into one's own skin: "Feeling one's worth, one's *infinite* worth." Bear suggested that each person needs to come home to their own heart, come home to the Great Heart—different ways of talking about the same thing, the essential thing: "Feeling at home. Here. As oneself."

When a person pursues an identity that may not be quite right for them, he said, "it's not the thing itself they want but the side benefits they imagine go with it—the respect or awards or money. Purity of purpose lies in wanting the thing itself, loving the activity rather than the things that go with it." Wanting side benefits could extend to something as subtle as wanting to find a place in the world. "One can even want the path," he said, "and yet within the wanting resides this deeper yearning to have a place in the world."

"You're talking about me, aren't you?" I said. I was beginning to recognize Bear's respectful, indirect way.

"It's bigger than just you," he replied. "The thing that needs to be addressed is a person's place in the world. One gets more solid in one's sense of place by following the way that's right for them, the very unique way."

Different people would come up against different challenges in trying to find their own place, he added. "For one person, it might mean treasuring the beauty of spirit within. For another, allowing oneself to be more comfortable in the physical world."

Then Bear paused. "For *you*," he said, "it might have to do with communion. Dwelling in the sense of back-and-forth."

A week or so later Bear returned to the theme of uniqueness. "Nature—reality—values individual variation," he said one morning. Then he repeated, "Nature loves yet another version. But not in the sense of a stale, repeated version. Something new. Something marvelous." One only has to look out the window, he suggested, to glimpse this flowering of endless variety.

All of nature's experimenting, Bear went on, adds up to a picture of continuously unfolding possibility. "It gives people the biggest freedom to pursue that which is theirs," he said. "Among the Helpers," he added, "there is a great respect for individuality."

11

As I groped my way forward in Journeys, I began to let go of trying too hard to figure them out and started to relax more easily into the communion. A feeling began to creep over me—a feeling that I had known how to do this long ago, that talking with unseen realms was familiar in some way that only the deepest-down, longest-buried part of me remembered. I was being delivered back to the land of my birth, back to my native tongue. It was a language I'd barely learned to speak before I'd been snatched away from it all too soon—by rows and files of desks in school, by trying to be like my friends, by succeeding in the work of the mind. My adult life, I was beginning to see, had been a story of exile.

It's not that as a child I enjoyed extraordinary experiences of communing in some special way with spirit. My experiences were the common kind, a moment here or there when the world discarded its usual garb and suddenly glowed in a new costume. Many children, perhaps all children, are shown such secrets. Some glimpse a shining world hidden just behind everyday sight or enjoy the feeling of being watched over by someone bigger than their parents. Some have an imaginary friend, like the comic strip character Calvin's stuffed tiger who, out of sight of other people, snaps to vivid life.

In my case, I rarely played with dolls and had only a few stuffed animals, none of which ever came alive for me. I never saw the shining world, at least as a child, and I couldn't quite place God either, though I did have the sense that the world is more mysterious than we know—that the birch tree in my yard might one day whisper secrets, that birds might be telling stories in their songs.

From time to time I enjoyed a dreamy state that I could sink into when the house was quiet, perhaps sitting beside a window on a rainy day and watching moisture gather into droplets on the glass, a droplet here or there growing heavier and heavier until suddenly it would slice downward, leaving behind a dotted line that soon melted away under other droplets, other lines, a tracery of moisture flowing down the glass. And when I was very small, I did occasionally hear on snowy nights something that seemed to my child-mind to be the whistle and moan of the winter wind in the electrical wires above our house. I listened with happiness: Who knew that the wires could sing such beautiful harmonies? The chords were sustained and rich; they went on for minutes at a time, resolving with unexpected turns. The music was haunting, unearthly.

Years later, an aptitude for music led me to enter college as a music major, and until I was thirty I toyed with the idea of becoming a professional musician. But music had been one of those puzzle pieces that almost but didn't quite fit; it required a little too much effort to push it into place. So I'd gone on to find my professional home among words, my other first love.

I'd learned to read at three or four years old, and from the time I could sound out words on the page I'd sought out books as if famished, starving. Throughout childhood books gave my imagination space to roam—to other times, other places, other ways of seeing and experiencing. As many hours as I could, every day, I lost myself in the landscape of books. But books also stole me away from the landscape beneath my own feet, the sensory world of tickling grasses and wiggling damp earthworms and the stiff brown clay that my older brother and I used to dig up from below the sandbox with our child-size shovels.

As I entered adulthood, reading became my ground, my solace, the center of my various professions. When people at parties asked what I did, I sometimes grinned and said, "I do books. I read them, edit them, teach them, and teach others how to write them."

Yet now as I explored communing with Bear, I found myself being encouraged to set aside time for letting my mind wander. Bear talked about a way of being that was bigger and more spacious than the intellect. One could think of the intellect as being pointed like a sharp object. This other way of being was amorphous, diffuse. It was the place of inspiration, the place of creativity and freedom— the heart center. It belonged on the same continuum, Bear said, as the place where we go after we die. Though most of us spend our everyday lives in pointed awareness, this more spacious place is accessible in every moment and can be reached at any time. "Nature is a true and certain avenue for contacting that spaciousness," Bear said. When one lives from that spacious place, life flows more easily, he added. One can see more clearly.

Bear said it would be important for me to recognize the difference between these two ways of being and, even more, to be able to cross the threshold between them with ease—to enter the spacious place at a moment's notice, day or night. The implication was clear. Up to now I had spent the vast majority of my life in the pointed mind, the intellect; now I needed practice dwelling in this other place.

Like many of the things Bear said in the early days, I heard the words, I spoke them into the phone recorder, I even typed them up later—and then I completely forgot about them, not comprehending.

This much I knew: I was being discouraged from doing work that required me to focus the mind in that old, pointed way on written words. In spite of Tim's and my tight finances, no new editing clients came my way that spring, which frightened me and at the same time filled me with relief because I didn't have the mental energy to concentrate on a new project. Bear seemed to be encouraging me to reacquaint myself with that dreamy state of childhood, to "let things go a little fuzzy," as he put it, to return to a half-remembered country where words were not yet crucial and knowledge flowed through other, more intimate, paths—through breath, and blood, and feeling.

I can't say that I relaxed into this advice. The truth is, I chafed at it. I grumbled about it to Tim and despaired of ever again finding my comfort zone. I experienced Bear's strategy for what it was—a taking apart of my accomplished adult self, piece by piece. But at the same time, I had to admit that letting go of the self I thought I knew seemed to be delivering me to a place I may have inhabited long, long ago. Even though I was leaving familiar territory, I sensed—I hoped—that I might be returning home.

12

April that year dipped frequently into cold and snow, six or eight or twelve inches of wet cement falling once a week, every week, throughout the month. A few days after each snowstorm, the ground would clear and the temperature rise to the sixties or seventies, the sun coaxing spring flowers into bloom and providing relief to residents weary of shoveling their walks. Then, a week later, more snow. The buyers of our house put theirs on the market, but I figured there was no need to think about moving just yet because no one would be shopping for houses in this weather.

Bear's words on April Fool's Day about "ebullient good enjoyment" turned out to be merely a warm-up for a whole series of conversations that snowy April about enjoying life. Bear brought it up in every Journey I engaged in that month. Every single one. I guess I needed a lot of reminding.

Bear recommended a particular flavor of enjoyment: "enjoying with no urge to change anything." (Who, me? Wanting to change things? Like, maybe, heavy snows for starters? Then, oh, I don't know, social inequality? And environmental madness?)

"There will always be things amiss," Bear said. "Finding enjoyment is not a matter of finding what's right in the world. When one feels that something is out of balance—and you *will* feel that, over and over—it's a good idea to return to the inner state of enjoyment." I kept wanting to use the word *acceptance,* but Bear wanted *enjoyment* instead.

"Go to that place of enjoyment, and start from there. Return to the place of no need to change anything, and then the ego is more out of the picture. It's when you *need* something to change that the mind and ego can come in and try to direct what is being changed. And when you let go and sink into the deeper place of the Great Heart, which is often signaled by a great peace with no need to change anything—when you start from that great peace, which looks like enjoyment—then the most wide-open changes, the most freedom-creating changes, the most magical, transformative changes can happen."

Bear said that such wide-open enjoyment is in fact love. "Root yourself in love," he said. "It's more about being deeply present to what-is." He added that it was a good practice to follow with every person in my life, since people can sniff out instantly when someone wants to change them. If I wished to avoid setting off someone's early warning system, enjoying them with no urge to change a thing was a good place to start. "The paradox," he said, "is that love, or enjoyment, is where change *can* arise from. It's one of the *few* places where change can arise from."

On another day Bear guided me through reflecting on some experiences in the past that I wasn't satisfied with—tough things that had consumed years of my life, the results of not-so-good decisions I'd made. Looking back, I wished I'd known better at the time.

Bear said not to worry about any of it, adding quietly, "There's no need for disquiet. No need." This was accompanied by a feeling that I was being wrapped in an enormous blanket of comfort.

"The mysteries run deeper than human beings can go," Bear said, bringing tears to my eyes. Better to regard each choice as a rung on the ladder taking me where I needed to go. "In this way one can approach even the past from that place of enjoying without feeling any urge to change. That is the best platform for living: to approach each moment—in the present, in the past—with appreciation. This provides the most resilience, the most elastic approach to living."

Appreciation, he said on another day, was the same thing as enjoying. Whether one was giving it or receiving it didn't matter; appreciation in either form worked the same magic. "It fills one's being. It gives one a sense of joyful fullness inside."

I asked, "What if someone is trying to practice appreciation for a situation that may not be good for them?"

He clarified: "Appreciation can be misdirected. Appreciating a bad situation is disempowering." He added, "Appreciation is enjoyment, remember. And enjoyment of a bad situation is negating one's own perception, tamping down and silencing one's own voice.

"Make sure the object of appreciation is worthy of appreciation," Bear went on. "The things most worthy of appreciation are living things." One can practice appreciating oneself, or one can appreciate and enjoy nature. "When appreciation grows for oneself," he said, "one grows beyond staying in a bad situation." Appreciating nature can clear the windows of perception so that a person can see their situation more clearly. "One can't go wrong in nature," he said, "in the great mysteries of the animals and plants and trees. When one is opened by experiencing that awe, then one can see where action is needed.

"Appreciate the life-force," he added, "in oneself, in another person, in a tree, animal, landscape, woods, the sea, mountains, rocks. Get in touch with *that*. Therein lies true life."

On yet another day, after I'd worked on a talk I was scheduled to give—why, oh, why had I thought I wanted to do so many of these talks?—Bear urged me to sit back and relax a little more. "It's mentally hard work to write a talk," he said. Taking time out to sit back and relax would help my body come back into balance. "Do what the body loves. Whatever helps enjoyment."

"Well, Bear," I replied, "in a time of change like this, it's a little hard to know what the body loves." I used to love sitting at my computer and concentrating on words, but what did I enjoy now? "What the body loves is going out birding," I added peevishly, "but it was too icy-windy-cold yesterday." I'd driven to one of my favorite birding spots, hoping to see the bald eagles who often hung out there, but the biting wind had forced me back into the car.

Bear was ever patient. He reminded me what I did after that— turned the car's heat on high while driving slowly along the country roads, scanning trees, birding by car. And that's when I came across a pasture filled with cows and a few young calves. One cow in particular, standing quietly apart from the others, drew my attention. I parked beside the road and raised my binoculars.

The cow stood still as a statue. A string of dark bloody tissue trailed to the ground beside her tail. At her feet lay a small calf, shining with moisture. As I watched, the calf raised its head and looked around. The cow gazed down without moving. The calf tested one leg, then another, then slowly stood up. After a few moments it walked around Mama and pushed its nose into her udder. She allowed the calf to nurse and then, with the little one beside her, began drifting back toward the others. I had just witnessed the first minutes of a brand-new life.

"Soooo," Bear said, "you found a way to enjoy from the warmth of your car, and you saw the freshly born calf. Modify the habits so that the body can enjoy. If being warm is what the body enjoys, then modify the habits so the body can feel warm—supported and cared for."

A week later Bear reminded me again about staying close to the body: "Always check in with the body. Move in alignment with what the body wants to do. That's the best basis for change."

I'd just returned from a book-reading trip to find in my inbox a last-minute invitation to speak on a panel at a big writers' conference in New York City that coming weekend. I would have to turn right around and board another plane. How could I possibly do that, already tired? But it was New York! How could I pass up an opportunity to slip for a few days into that buzzing hubbub of vitality?

Bear advised, "If it makes one ignore the needs of the body, the needs of the everyday, then it's a taxing path rather than a life-giving one. Choose what is life-giving."

He added, "If one doesn't say yes to one's own body, how can one expect to say yes to the world, to the body of Earth, the bodies of other creatures?"

13

During April the Journey process filled a great deal of my time, for in addition to spending twenty or thirty or fifty minutes almost every day in a conversation with Bear, I was trying to transcribe each session as well, which took twice that long. Between Journeys and typing, I might meet on the phone with my few remaining editing clients and then plan the details of the next workshop, the next trip. The shakiness from some weeks ago had passed, but now I felt like an astonished visitor to the world, needing to pay close attention to find my way around in this new land because it didn't operate quite like my old one.

Even when traveling I set aside time for Journeys, mumbling softly into my phone recorder in the privacy of a guest bedroom or a basement. Bear, I discovered, was ready to offer advice about leading a workshop, and his suggestions always settled me closer to the heart.

"The communion is the thing they come for," Bear observed as I prepared for a writing workshop in North Carolina. Keeping close to that warm heart of communion, he added, would allow the workshop to speak to people in the best possible way.

Early on the morning of the workshop, huddled under the covers in my friend's house in Durham, I thought about all the prep work now completed. I'd considered every minute of the three-hour time, juggling the segments once, then again, for the best possible experience. I'd talked through the lineup, timing each anecdote. I felt prepared. The workshop was ready to go.

Even so, I asked Bear if he had anything more to show me about it.

In response, I saw an image of Bear's head with his jaw wide open, two sets of bear teeth gleaming. They were huge! And sharp! Bear was pointing to his enormous teeth.

What could he mean? I had no idea. Puzzled, I asked if he could show me something to shed light on that picture. Then I glimpsed people in a room playing with an inflatable plastic ball, like a big balloon, batting it up in the air over here, over there, all around the room. Having fun.

This made no sense whatsoever. I figured I must be seeing things—mind wandering, a little jangled from traveling. But I was beginning to learn that images from Bear didn't always make sense in quite the way I expected them to. So to give Bear a chance, I asked, "What could this possibly have to do with your teeth?"

Instantly Bear's quiet thought came: "And what happens if you sink these teeth into a ball like that?"

Easy. "Well, it will burst. It will deflate, just like that."

"Sharp teeth are for when you mean business," Bear said. "If the topic is light, they have to be used lightly."

Finally I got it. I needed to have more fun with the workshop, not let it get in any way heavy or wordy. Just enjoy!

That afternoon I cut out most of what I intended to say. I told people not to take the process too seriously—that if they found themselves working a bit hard, just to mentally sit back and enjoy a little more. I watched shoulders loosen and smiles break out around the room. A feeling of zest and warmth then filled our time together.

"Keep enjoying!" Bear said later.

Of course.

"One's movement is most pure and effortless when it comes from that enjoyment," he added.

On a different morning of that same trip, feeling off-balance from too much motion and too little sleep, I reflected on how I'd been looking forward to a touch of warmth and bright blooming flowers in North Carolina. Spring was supposed to be here by now! Instead, all I'd seen so far were low gray skies and chilly rain.

"It's really faith you're after, isn't it?" Bear observed.

I thought I was after warmer weather.

"It's faith you're after," Bear repeated. Faith, he said, was a deep sense of the rightness in the world. He added, "Enjoyment is the quickest route to faith."

I paused. "Did I get that right?" I'd never heard things put in quite that order before.

"Enjoyment is the most direct way to balance," Bear responded, "to feeling the deep rightness, which is faith. Enjoyment is a direct line to faith."

Outside the window a bird called and whistled in a voice I didn't recognize. Later that morning, as I walked through the rolling woodsy hills of the neighborhood during a break in the rain, I spotted the noisy singer. A cardinal, oh, joy! In my childhood their scarlet cloaks had leaped from snowy yards, but now, with binoculars, I could study them up close. Such fat, bright red beaks! On brownish females it popped like a Christmas tree light. Such vivid red feathers! And raucous calls! I listened and watched, absorbed. And when I returned to the house, I felt steadier, calmer.

"This is how one soothes the tummy and calms the nervous system," Bear said. "Just keep dropping into enjoyment. Robust enjoyment."

Later in the week the skies cleared, and before I left Durham I enjoyed rhododendrons bursting into magenta and fruit trees draped in white lace.

Back home again, one morning I asked, "Is enjoyment the theme for today?"

"It's the learning of a lifetime!" Bear replied cheerfully.

14

Tim and I sometimes laughed, when I reported a detail from a Journey with Bear, "We never learned *that* in Sunday school!" Never was this more true than in Bear's encouragement to enjoy life. Our sober Mennonite forebears were earnest and sincere—diligent in work as well as in prayer. Though they loved to quietly tease and joke, I never saw anyone my parents' age or older break into boisterous laughter, at least not in public. My mother, when she laughed aloud, covered her mouth with one hand as if ashamed. I grew up being as serious as the best of them.

Yet if Bear was teaching an enjoyment I'd never learned from my elders, he often sounded remarkably like the Jesus my elders had followed—the Jesus who enjoyed hanging out with children, who stopped his too-earnest followers from shooing the children away, who said that the kingdom of heaven could be found only by becoming like a child. He'd also said, "The kingdom of heaven is within you," a sentence that is just as accurately translated, "The kingdom of heaven is among you." That more spacious place is here. Right now. Inside you, around you, in your midst. It only requires a shift to experience it. This same Jesus had partied with social misfits when his followers wanted him to cultivate more respectable contacts.

He'd said that God is a loving parent who cares so much about the intimate details of life that even the fall of a sparrow—a sparrow so worthless it was sold in the market for half a penny—is noticed and held in divine love.

I remembered too a Sufi teacher I'd met years before, a round-ish, unassuming man from Turkey named Sherif Baba whose dark-brown eyes were always shining. A decade earlier, in Berkeley, I'd even attended *sohbet* with Baba, a traditional Sufi teaching session in which people gather around the master and listen to his stories. That afternoon twenty or so of us had lined a makeshift, unfurnished room, sitting on cushions with our backs against the walls. Baba told simple parables, everyday stories, a few sentences at a time translated by his companion. I wondered what was so special about *sohbet*—and about Baba—until I noticed that Baba's attention was shifting to a different person every few minutes. Glancing repeatedly at my friend who had invited me, Baba was telling a parable about a farmer who, on his way to market with his harvest of grain, hears of a valuable treasure. The farmer promptly leaves his cart of grain where it is, sacrificing all his hard work, because he knows that what he will find instead is priceless. My friend was watching Baba closely, smiling but also thinking, evaluating, a little wary. Baba was only telling stories, but something deeper was happening.

Then Baba began talking quietly about how life has a way of handing us things we don't expect—some pleasant, some not so pleasant. Even very bitter things can happen, such as losing people or relationships that mean a great deal to us. Baba now was looking at me. "It's very important to let go of things when it's time for them to go," the translator said.

I looked down, nodding. My intimate relationship of five years with the man with whom I co-owned a house was on the rocks, and I knew without knowing that it would soon end.

Baba went on: "Every experience in life holds a little bit of its opposite. Every sweetness in life holds a bitterness, and every bitterness holds a sweetness. When you go through a bitterness, find the thing hiding within it. Find the sweetness in the bitterness."

Baba had been right. Within a month of that meeting, my relationship had ended, which over the next couple of years had led to the wrenching decision to leave my Oakland home. During the leaving I'd kept Baba's words nearby, looking for sweetness. It hadn't taken long to arrive. Only a few months later I'd reconnected with Tim, whom I'd met at eighteen—a momentous sweetness lifted straight out of those bitter wrappings.

Having spent time with Bear, I now understood Baba a little better. Baba's shining eyes, his way of talking quietly with love— they reminded me a lot of Bear and of his gentle, down-to-earth manner, of the warm cloak that wrapped me in its shelter. Baba had known what to say to each person because he was listening. His Sufi order, after all, had been founded by the great twelfth-century poet Rumi, who had opened his most famous book, the *Masnavi*, with that exact word: "Listen." Baba liked to say that the real divine wisdom is to listen to yourself, to that deep wisdom in your own center.

Bear too had a lot to say about listening; he called it the foundation for this new life I was building. "Meet each situation with listening," Bear advised, especially when I was speaking with a group of people. "Always settle in the heart; always check against compassion. There is *nothing* firmer than that, in the sense that in this shifting world, one can't *get* firmer than that." The best guide, always, would be to ask, Is my heart open in compassion to this moment? To this person, these people, in front of me? To my Helper? "That is the best you can do," Bear said. "That is the *very* best you can do. That is the way a little crack of openness can get bigger over time."

15

Bear talked a lot about being open. He urged me to cultivate a simple, open frame of mind at all times. "Simplicity," he said one morning, "looks like a humble station from the point of view of the noisier parts of the world."

Just the night before I'd done a radio show in which the interviewer was forever taking off into Big Stories and Universal Truths. I'd felt like a herd dog trying to bring the attention back to something simple and nourishing—like Bodhi nudging me patiently, over and over, toward the kitchen, where an empty soup pot is cooling on the counter so he can lick it clean.

"There are places and times," Bear said, "when what is simple and open is regarded as too simple—and thus foolish. In those places and times, it's better to be foolish." Bear added, "Don't be afraid to come back to what is simple and open because that's where the voice of spirit, the heart, the Great Heart—whatever you want to call the bigger voice—is found. It is heard as a very still, small voice. That's a good test of authenticity. Not bombastic, not certain, in that mental way of being certain. Not flying high. But calm and simple."

Being open at the start of a Journey, I was discovering, allowed the Journey to unfold in the clearest possible way. Any strong emotion I was feeling got in the way of a conversation with Bear, shutting down the easy flow of communion. Irritability, discontent, dissatisfaction with life, dreading things to come—each of them obscured the Helper's presence. On days that I felt them, my sense of Bear would fade and a sense of vacancy would follow.

But just as unhelpful were overexcitement, eagerness, a feeling of "this is so cool!—I've gotta do it!" Strong pleasant emotions would equally get in the way of hearing the Helper. Bear suggested they "can sound very good but again take one further away from that small quiet point of openness." If I wanted to hear from a source wiser than me, I simply had to let go of how I wanted things to be. I had to be just as willing to hear Bear recommend the opposite of what I wanted as I was to having him agree with me. I had to approach a neutral frame of mind.

For me this was not easy. Not in the least. Bear wouldn't have needed to talk to me about things that were easy.

I began paying more attention to my unspoken wishes, trying to discern any leaning toward left or right. I prepared for a Journey with Bear by taking a step or two back from all fixed ways of thinking, back toward neutral. Only then would I be open enough to receive images or words that I didn't expect. I was glad for some training in mindfulness—many hours spent observing thoughts, watching them come and go.

When, after bracketing my own wishes about how I wanted things to be, I actually sat down and consulted with Bear, I was often in for a surprise. Bear might place all the options in a bigger frame. Or Bear might show me something else entirely, for instance, a countryside scene with beautiful pastures, where he might invite me to open the gate I was standing behind and walk outside the fence so I could appreciate a more panoramic view.

"The neutral place is the loving place," Bear said. "It's a matter of just being willing."

Could it be that life was really that simple?

16

The last of the heavy spring snows arrived that year on May 1, a day I was to do a signing at a local bookstore. I'd chosen the date months before because it fell after snow season. But that day eight inches of snow covered the ground by midafternoon with more coming down, and I canceled the signing.

The heavy spring snows that year also delayed the start of my summer volunteer job, monitoring bluebird nestboxes on Bald Mountain. Tim and I had long loved Bald Mountain, a small cone-shaped hill five miles outside of Boulder. We often spent Sunday mornings packing Bodhi into the car, driving twenty minutes through curvy mountain roads, and hiking the short steep trail to the bench at the top. There Bodhi would scratch a hole for himself in the dirt under the bench while Tim and I scooted close together above him and gazed east—toward the backsides of the Flatirons, those enormous tilted slabs of sandstone at the edge of town, their tips almost at eye level, and toward the city of Boulder spread out sparkling in the valley below. On the mountain we talked slowly, easily. The deeper currents of our hearts emerged on that bench.

Three years earlier, the enormous Fourmile Fire of Labor Day week had blazed through miles of land, burning houses to the ground before racing up the backside of Bald Mountain. There it had decimated a thick ponderosa forest growing around one ancient tree, a six-hundred-year-old giant with a massive trunk and gnarled, heavy limbs that curled back on themselves as they circled toward the sky. This tree had been a seedling while the Aztecs built an empire and Gutenberg fiddled with movable type. It had seen dozens of fires, perhaps fifty or sixty all told, and it knew what to do with fire. Old ponderosas simply slough off their scaly shreds of outer bark when they get singed, carrying the fire's heat away from the tree.

As we always did when we hiked Bald Mountain, on the day before Labor Day we had paused on the trail above the old ponderosa while I scrambled down to place my hands for a few moments on its sturdy trunk, to sniff the hint of butterscotch in the cracks of its thick, fire-safe bark, to lean my shoulder against its humming life. That Sunday turned out to be one of the last days of its life.

By Wednesday, the Fourmile File had leveled everything in its path. A century of fire suppression had resulted in a forest that was too thick and a fire that, instead of thinning out the trees, destroyed them completely. The Fourmile Fire was a conflagration.

As soon as the ground cooled, safety crews cut the old ponderosa down, and its twisted limbs lay along the charred hillside, light reflecting off the prisms of their fire-shiny charcoal bark. I wondered how the tree had looked as it blazed upward—six hundred years of fires in its memory, but this fire the one that finally claimed it for the sky, for the earth.

Visiting Bald Mountain after the Fourmile Fire had been an exercise in prayer—in remembering that dying makes way for new life, in being grateful for both moments. Eagerly we'd watched the mountain recover—different wildflowers the following spring than we'd seen before but also the familiar ones, more thrilling than usual. Lavender pasqueflower dotting the mountain's singed northern slope. Bunches of cacti, burned to the ground without a trace, sending up tender, prickly new shoots. The fire had spared our favorite bench at the top, and in the three years since then, its varnished wooden slats had lost their patina of splashed blood—the rust-colored flame retardant dropped by pilots flying pass after pass over the mountain as they tried to hold the fire line at its peak.

My nestbox-monitoring job had begun just the year before—yet another way I'd bonded with Bald Mountain. Eight bluebird nestboxes had been tacked to ponderosas on the sunny southeastern slope, a several-acre stretch closed to the public and untouched by the fire. Monitoring involved visiting the boxes every few days during nesting season. I would hike cross-country up and down the steep, grassy slope; find the trees with boxes—not so easy on a tall hillside where all the ponderosas look exactly alike; then open each box and use a small mirror on a stick, like the ones dentists use, to peek inside.

I'd learned that pygmy nuthatches arrive in the spring earlier than bluebirds, that they claim their boxes first and defend them fiercely. Pygmy nuthatches are tiny birds, but the previous spring, every time I checked their box, they were bundles of indignation, scolding and dive-bombing my head so that I'd taken to wearing a hat with a sturdy brim to protect my eyes. Then later in the summer, after all eight of their chicks had fledged, I had visited their box one last time. Though family duties were over, one of the parents began sounding an alarm as I approached and followed me nervously over-head. I sat down under a ponderosa a short distance away from their tree to catch my breath, and when I did, the nuthatch above me quit fluttering and perched twenty or so feet directly over my head. Suddenly I realized what might be happening. I glanced up then shifted quickly to my right, just in time to hear the splat of bird poop on my left sleeve.

This spring, though the bluebirds set up housekeeping later than usual, the pygmy nuthatches moved in on time, apparently unfazed by the snow. By mid-May, when I took up my usual circuit, violet-green swallows too had arrived and were circling the sky in the vicinity of the box they'd occupied the previous year. But as I headed toward their tree one morning I heard a raven fifty feet farther up the hill croaking loudly. Spotting the raven, I saw that it was staring downhill directly at me. I wheeled and headed in the opposite direc-tion, working my way backward through the boxes, which took twice as long since I didn't know my way up and down the mountainside from this angle.

My evasive maneuvers were futile; ravens are not so easily fooled. That box did get attacked later, its contents reduced to two tiny newborn bodies mangled and desiccated by the time I found them. Everybody needs to eat, I reminded myself; it had been a lean and snowy spring for all. But why couldn't that raven have eaten all it killed? At least the snakes were tidier, leaving no trace of their visits. A box that one week housed a nest full of eggs or newborns might be completely abandoned the following, clean and dry, without so much as a blade of nest grass out of place. I wanted snake guards on these boxes, for the snakes on this hillside knew exactly where to find the reliable buffets that so conveniently filled up year after year with their favorite treats. (Snake guards did go up after that season.)

This year the pygmy nuthatches worked in stealth, filling their boxes in secret with grassy nests and eggs, then disappearing every time I came around. In early June I visited one box of chicks in the middle of hatching—six squirmy, wobbly necked, dime-size babies in the nest with two remaining eggs that looked translucent, as if liquid life could spill out at any moment, bursting.

In the other nuthatch box that day, naked nestlings slept soundly, not quite here yet, as if they still slumbered within their eggs. I wondered if they were dead, but no, they were fleshy, pink, warm—seven of them in a downy cup barely two inches across, a pile of miniature naked joints and bulging bluish eyelids. The eighth lay a half inch away. I stretched out a tentative index finger to brush it ever so lightly. It did not stir. Was it dying? Or preparing to live? I couldn't tell. The sight of the babies felt shocking, almost like the sight of dying; they had come so brand-new into the world.

But bluebirds that summer were scarce. The deep snows of early spring had been too much for them. Later I learned that bluebirds winter near Albuquerque, where freezing temperatures and snow are daily facts of winter life. So it wasn't the cold that did them in, or the snow per se. It was the depth of the snow—snow covering the ground, obscuring all food, making it impossible for them to forage. Many bluebirds that spring had likely starved.

Other birds didn't fare so well either that summer; few of the babies who hatched in the boxes graduated to the sky. Still, I enjoyed trudging up and down the grassy slope, having the mountain to myself except for the occasional car on the nearby road, listening to the calls of flickers and chipping sparrows and the whooshing of wind in pines, admiring tall lavender penstemon as the season progressed and tangerine-tinged golden cups of cactus blooms, staying alert for glimpses of vivid blue wings flashing between trees.

At home at my desk I could barely read anything, not even the books my friends were publishing, manuscripts that I'd known and loved for several years while they were being written. But during every two-hour trip to Bald Mountain I could read the land. It was a way of communing that had long been familiar, this way of loving through the senses. It took me to the heart, to that more spacious place, as filling the senses always does. It was another way of listening.

17

Who was I listening to when I talked with Bear? My own center or a being outside me? Though I suspected the question was pointless, I asked it anyway.

I wanted to think of spiritual help as coming from inside us. Early in my adult life I'd become disillusioned with the far-off God of Protestantism who gazed down as an overseer from his remote heaven. My feminist awakening in college had dislodged God from that massive throne simply by teaching me to pay attention to my own body. Suddenly my eyes had been opened to just how deep the habit went in Western Christendom of regarding the self and the body and everything earthly as imperfect, as not-God. It diminished all physical life. The God-up-there also nicely reinforced the hierarchical arrangements of human power, as if some people just naturally deserved obedience or privileges. In seminary I'd studied feminist theology, experimenting with ways of picturing the world that placed God among us instead of above us. By the time I left the church, later in my twenties, my center of authority was lodged firmly within myself, and my sense of God—though I wasn't very comfortable using the word anymore—had a lot to do with connection and love and the ground beneath our feet.

In my thirties, serious illness and overwhelming loss had led me to seek healing in nature, and I had spent the rest of my adult life discovering that nature speaks with countless voices. I'd gone against the view that human minds alone hold intelligence, and I'd written a book about the depths of connection we can enjoy with a tree, a dog, or a creek when we're willing to hear the songs of other creatures.

So why did I still want the wisdom to emerge from within me? It was a good question. In a real sense the wisdom did; hearing my Helper's voice involved, every time, getting quiet, clearing busyness and mental agendas out of the way, being open to what Bear might want to bring to my attention that day. It was a practice that took me to my own center.

But Bear was clearly not "me." Because Tim knew me so well, he was sensitive to the difference. He said, when I reported a joke from Bear, that it was not my humor; it reminded him of my older brother, a trucker who loved country music, wore loud Hawaiian shirts, and dragged his friends into karaoke bars—and sang in them—every chance he could get. I too was surprised by the "otherness" of Bear. The thoughts that arose during Journeys were not my thoughts; they stretched me, gave me ways of thinking that I'd never considered before. They often surprised me.

But I had to give Bear this: It was precisely his otherness that made our relationship possible. It provided someone to talk to. It gave me a sense of being cared for. It offered a feeling of camaraderie, like someone walking beside me, a hand lightly touching my elbow to steady me over uneven ground. Life was easier than I had imagined because I didn't have to do all the work myself.

I asked Bear one day why, in Journeys, he sometimes showed up as a bear and sometimes as a more amorphous presence, like a feeling of support.

"The form doesn't matter," Bear replied. "What matters is opening to a larger point of view." Because the Helper belongs to that spacious place of the heart—dwelling there more consistently than a human being can—the Helper is equipped to offer wisdom that cannot be gained from merely a part of the human self. "What matters is the opening," Bear said. "Consulting with a larger point of view."

Bear seemed to think that my talking with him differed little from communing with a tree in my yard or with Bodhi, who liked to snuggle on the sofa next to me, rolling onto his back so I could rub his belly. Just because I couldn't see Bear with physical eyes didn't mean that he was any less real or alive or that he had any less ability to interact with me. This relationship was meant to smooth my passage through life; seeing it as ethereal or otherworldly would tend to limit its helpfulness.

"It is not that far away from the rest of the parts of the person," Bear said. "It works in tandem with all the parts of the person. It brings a person back to center, the bigger center of themselves."

If I was tempted to view Bear as "supernatural" because he belonged to an other-than-physical world, while Bodhi and the tree in my yard were "natural," Bear had one brief and quiet thing to say: "It's not necessary to divide things up that way."

18

One morning in May, Bear called my attention to things that were preoccupying me—a deadline for an online essay, a road trip to a conference in a few days, the usual responsibilities. No wonder I wasn't feeling much connection with my Helper at the moment.

"When the mind is full of other responsibilities, other treasures," Bear said, "it's harder to be aware of the treasures coming from the Helper."

"Okay, so how do I hold those responsibilities more lightly?" I asked. We were getting down to a place I was a little reluctant to go. "I'd rather have this conversation be all about fun and enjoyment," I added.

"Perhaps it is," Bear said. He added simply, "Not to let the things of life take over."

"Is that it, Bear? Not to be taken over by the demands of life?"

"Not to the point of obscuring your connection to the deep pleasure of the world," Bear replied. "That deep joy is a lifeline. Hold on to the lifeline, the deep joy."

A few weeks later, some travel completed and responsibilities fulfilled, when I asked Bear what he might have for the day, Bear said, "Notice how your state of mind shifts when you get in touch with your Helper." Bear asked me to describe the shift.

"Lighthearted," I said immediately. "Even comical. It's always more simple and clear. A more loving, amused attention toward life."

"Treasure that state of mind," Bear responded. "When you feel a heavier state of mind, it's a good idea to come here and talk with Bear." Then Bear instantly appeared in suspenders and a skirt.

I chuckled. "Is that your dancing skirt, Bear?"

"Just being silly," Bear responded. "Lighthearted." Then he added, "Lithe-hearted. A lighthearted frame of mind helps one move through the world in a lithe way."

19

I was grateful that Tim enjoyed hearing about Bear, for with many other friends I felt that I was taking chances. Some were wonderfully supportive, like the friend who, when I sucked in a deep breath and told her that I'd embarked on a shamanic path and how surprised I was about it, endeared herself forever when she burst out laughing and said, "You mean you didn't know?" Other friends might listen without comment and never bring it up again, as if they wished this part of me to stay politely hidden. Still others withdrew completely, edging away month by month, even if we'd been close for years.

But Tim offered unfailing support. He was ready to hear as much or as little as I wished to share with him about what I was experiencing, and he listened with respect and kindness. Sometimes his eyes flickered with longing, and I suspected that some part of him deeply wished for a similar path.

One night he asked what going on a Journey with a Helper was like.

"It's maddeningly simple," I found myself saying. "It's just opening, moment by moment, to what's happening."

It was maddening just because it was so simple. What could be easier than following the impressions that flowed across one's awareness when the eyes were closed?

In those early weeks and months, most of the Journeys unfolded like conversations. This was comfortable for me, a person who had made her living with words. Sometimes a visual image would appear and occasionally the feeling of being in a small movie, like the train I had felt beneath me during those first conversations with Bear. Sometimes other sense impressions appeared—a taste, a smell, a feeling, a color. Journeys could include any of these languages of the heart. Sometimes images or sense impressions were connected to words, sometimes not.

The important thing in each Journey was that I let Bear take the lead; I opened to a perspective larger than my own. If I began the Journey with the sincere intention of following my Helper's wisdom—in other words, of opening to the highest good—then I could trust that the impressions or images or words that appeared were being communicated by the Helper and had something to offer. It was my job to simply notice them and speak them.

Though meditating had sharpened my ability to watch impressions passing moment to moment through the mind, this path was different from most mindfulness or Buddhist paths. The difference—and it was a big one—was that here the impressions were not something to be noticed and then let go of. They were instead the main event. They had been given by an other-than-human companion, a Helper. If I accepted those impressions or images as gifts, I could receive sustenance and insight. I could experience a two-way relationship.

My mind decided many times that watching the impressions unfold was entirely too simple. Over and over it inserted itself to help—assessing images, sifting and discarding impressions, offering explanations and judgments. One of its favorite lines was intended to address my naïveté: "You're just making this up." Except the message was trickier than that, for it always showed up in first person: "I must be making this up; it can't be true." Or if, during a Journey, an image appeared that made no sense at all, I would hear myself quickly think, "My attention must be wandering; this is just a distraction." If what I heard from the Helper sounded familiar, like something I might say, the great Master of Mutual Exclusiveness in my mind would instantly decide, "That sounds like me talking, so it can't be the Helper." If the images I sensed were cloudy or unclear, the mind was ready to place all the responsibility on me: "I must be off today; I'm just not seeing well."

Over time I began to realize that this path required me to trust my own perception to a radical degree—more than I'd ever trusted it before. I needed to be able to coax each of those elusive impressions out from the shadows and simply notice and name them. A calm confidence in what I perceived was key. Once those fleeting impressions had surrendered to the spotlight, I could then ask my Helper if they belonged in the Journey or not: Was this just a case of my mind wandering, or was it something more? Bear was happy to oblige with, for instance, a "getting colder" feeling or a "let's take it a little further" message.

Bear had the most fun on days when my mind quickly dismissed as "not the Helper" anything that I suspected was coming from my own self. Bear chuckled at such either-or judgments. As usual, he brought it back to enjoyment. "One can notice the difference between one's own wisdom and the wisdom of the Helper," Bear said, but "the goal is to keep them close together so that the two worlds do not run on separate tracks." Then Bear added, "Integrating them is what allows one to dwell in joy. Enjoyment is the start; begin there. It is also the goal, achieved by integrating the voice of the Helper into one's own everyday life."

This was a day when Bear was emphasizing how close the Helper's voice may be to one's own—so close that it might even be appropriate to call the Helper's voice "I." "Because," Bear said, "it is, after all, the source of the I. It is the deep source. When people find their own true voice, they are finding the source of the I."

That day I'd just come from lunch with a new acquaintance who was also following a shamanic path, but she talked about her path as one of channeling, a term that had set my teeth on edge— from the start of the curry and rice right through to the sweet curds and tea. Though I had never attended a channeling session, I had talked with others who had. They gave the impression of listening to disembodied, spooky entities who might or might not be speaking in love or working for the highest good. I asked Bear about that word.

"It is good to be wary of the term *channeling*," Bear replied, "because it communicates a feeling of separation and distance between the everyday and the Helper's calm, abiding voice. When what people need," Bear added, filling my awareness with the smell of a rich soup simmering for an afternoon on the stove, "is more like stewing in the voice of the Helper, allowing it to cook within them- selves, allowing themselves to be cooked with it, so that it all blends into a tasty and nourishing stew."

20

May in Boulder brought dandelions, along with another volunteer job I had inadvertently created for myself the previous spring. Those cheery blankets of yellow blooms offended the green-lawn aesthetic of many people and led to widespread pesticide use throughout town. Though pesticides had been phased out of city parks several years before, and here and there neighbors were banding together and pledging not to use pesticides in their yards, and though organic dandelion greens were being sold in the trendy supermarket a few blocks away for many dollars a bunch, my neighbors went on spraying. I'd been horrified to find, when we moved onto this street five years before, that every year those little orange plastic warning flags sprouted on the common lawn in the middle of the cul-de-sac managed by the homeowners' association. Every year the pesticides flowed.

One spring I'd circulated a petition to stop the pesticides. It had been voted down by the HOA board. Many of the residents had shared this street for forty years, longer than I could imagine. On just about every issue they disagreed vehemently—and had for decades—straight down party lines, but on dandelions they saw completely eye to eye: those awful weeds had to go, by any means possible. Stalwart Democrats favored pesticides as much as staunch Republicans.

The previous year I'd taken a cue from a volunteer gardening group at Chautauqua, the huge city park tucked under the Flatirons at the edge of town. In the native plant garden at Chautauqua, when three or four or five of us sat down together pulling cheatgrass or thinning overgrown flowers, tongues loosened. Conversation flowed. One day we might talk about evolution, the next alternative medicine—things we didn't normally discuss with strangers. We allowed ourselves to do it here because we were planted side by side with our hands in the dirt, making a garden happen together. What if that camaraderie could take place on my street?

So the previous May I'd organized some weekend dandelion-pulling parties on the common lawn with the help of a key neighbor. (As a newcomer to the street and a renter, I could get away with this.) The parties had been a huge success. One of them had even ended in a brunch on an HOA board member's patio with a dozen people laughing and joking and nibbling strawberries around a table. The fact that something was being done about dandelions had convinced the board to lay off on the pesticides for at least a year.

This spring, I found, momentum was on our side. Neighbors now expected the dandelion-pulling parties and asked when they would begin. Signs of spring thaw were popping up on the street in other ways as well. Regular yoga classes now took place at the community clubhouse, offered for free by one of the residents. Another neighbor had organized an art show and reception to display the talents of both amateurs and pros on this block. The old party lines, if not softening, at least seemed less pronounced.

As I hauled a basket and a dandelion puller across the street to the common lawn, I reflected on this way of making change. It matched the spirit that Bear had recommended, of being rooted in fun, in enjoyment. This year, when a few of us bent over the grass to pull dandelions, we talked like crazy. We told stories and laughed often. We acted silly. And the board again held off on pesticides.

But Bear had more to say about dandelions. Some days later, as I knelt in my own yard weeding, Bear began to chuckle at that term, *weeding*. Such a slippery term, a name for something that doesn't exist except in human minds! Bear suggested I notice the soil. He whispered that the soil knows which plants to attract for the health of that particular place.

My postage-stamp yard, like all the lawns on the street, had been planted with Kentucky bluegrass, the standard lawn turf. Kentucky blue is the pasture grass of a damper, cooler world. It is native to Europe and Asia and grows well in moist, cool climates such as the Northeast. When it has plenty of water, Kentucky blue creates a nice, thick, uniform grass above ground.

But the roots of Kentucky blue belong in mud; they stretch barely two or three inches into the soil. By contrast, most of the plants native to the high, dry prairies of Colorado grow roots that stretch at least a foot—and maybe ten or fifteen feet—into the ground. Their impossibly long root systems are needed both to reach the all-too-elusive moisture and to stabilize the soil so it doesn't blow away in the strong winds sweeping down off the Rockies.

As I bent over the grass in my yard, I saw that the dandelions and other so-called weeds I was pulling had longer or more intricately webbed roots than Kentucky blue. Could Bear be right? Could it be that the ground itself was inviting those longer-rooted plants to come settle in this dry, windy place? Did the soil itself know?

"It's a partnership," Bear said, "a collaboration between the soil and the plants to keep the land healthy." He added, "As long as there is Kentucky blue here, there will be dandelions. It's a communal affair."

His words reminded me of the knee surgery I'd undergone some years before to replace a torn ligament. A surgeon took a piece of tendon tissue and inserted it into the space formerly occupied by the ligament. Though tendons, unlike ligaments, have few blood vessels in them, after a few short weeks this tendon tissue began growing its own blood vessels as if it were a ligament—just because it now resided in the slot of a ligament. The body knew exactly what kind of tissue belonged where. Was it possible such intelligence extended to the ground itself?

21

During May I started to feel at loose ends again. This path had been unfolding for two intense months, and yet I felt no nearer to knowing what my purpose was or how to find it. Maybe it was the first relationship crisis with Bear. It felt familiar—that period of time, six or eight weeks in to a new relationship, when you pause and wonder if this is really the direction you want to be going and the person you want to be going there with.

I'd heard writers say that there were at least two ways to write a novel: You could plot the events and plan the characters ahead of time so you knew exactly what was going to happen throughout the book. Or you could just start at the beginning and then keep going with no idea at all of how it was going to turn out. A writing teacher I knew called it "following the image"—watching your characters tell their story, allowing their movie to unroll in your head. In life I'd always figured it was safer to plan and plot, though most of the time I'd ended up feeling my way along after all—and having a much better time because of it. But now I was having to follow the image so literally during each Journey that I had to laugh—when I wasn't grinding my teeth in frustration because the way felt so uncertain. I was impatient to know where I was going.

In response, Bear set me back on the train that we'd been traveling on in March during our very first conversations. This time Bear was wearing a train engineer's hat and staring fixedly ahead. Seeing a bear in an engineer's hat would have been funny except I wasn't feeling very humorous at the time—and Bear was staring ahead with an intensity I hadn't seen in him before. Our train barreled down the tracks, its horn blowing loudly at each of the little hamlets flashing by the windows.

"Don't get distracted," Bear said. "The feeling of barreling forward is to clarify that it's a kind of momentum that can keep one from being distracted by inconsequential things along the way. Blow by the towns where a stop isn't called for. Tap in to that sense of purpose, *even if* you don't know what the purpose entails." Bear stared at the tracks ahead of us. "This is a time to be steadfast. To follow the tracks where they lead."

Bear did offer one clue: "Your purpose is related to following the openings you find that are the most thrilling, comfortable, satisfying, comfortable." Bear had repeated the word *comfortable* on purpose. "Keep your eye on the activities that help you feel good. Blow by all the others."

22

By the end of May, Bear was suggesting that this Journey process could get more complicated and subtle, and to be prepared for that. "Keep your feet on the ground by keeping your senses tuned to *this* world," Bear advised.

It wasn't hard to fill the senses during spring, with grasses growing lush and green on the Rocky Mountain foothills outside our windows and the brilliant orange of Bullock's orioles freshly returned from Mexico flashing through the yard. Several weeks earlier I'd glimpsed the first one while writing an article on urban birding. At the very moment when I was typing lines about looking for orioles each spring, a pine branch just outside the window quivered, and I turned to spot a deep-orange male with black goatee pausing there. I rushed to pull the oriole feeder from winter storage and fill it with sugar water, adding large dollops of grape jelly in the receptacles on the lid.

These orioles apparently knew just where to look for the feeder. Within minutes a half dozen of them filled my tiny enclosed patio, perching on branches or on the ground, panting, then taking turns one by one at the feeder, gulping grape jelly. I saw a couple of mature males in orange and black with splashy white wing patches, a few olive-colored females with dark wings, and a yellow-olive first-year male with a black goatee—probably a family group just arrived, exhausted, from their trip.

I felt a special bond with orioles, for decades before, in Oakland, a newly hatched hooded oriole who fell from his nest in a palm tree far above had helped start me on this journey of connecting with the more-than-human world. After I rescued that baby, a tiny male, he had gone on to thrive and eventually be released from a rehab center, and his success had inspired me to later volunteer in a wildlife rehab hospital, where I had learned how to feed baby birds, how to treat bird and mammal injuries, how to raise baby opossums—yet more ways of bridging the gaps between me and the rest of nature.

I was glad that orioles abounded at our end of Boulder. They loved to hang their pendulous nests a few blocks away in the enormous cottonwoods next to a small urban lake, then fly to our street for grape jelly. My summer days were organized around orioles. I often woke just after dawn to their hoarse chatter and squeaky calls and stumbled out of bed right away to hang their feeder (we brought it in at night to discourage raccoons). The orioles stopped at our house many times every day, though they were cagier than most birds, lifting instantly off the feeder if a human appeared closer than twenty feet away, even through glass. I often snuck around walls and doorways to catch close-up glimpses of them. Orioles were my favorite part of summer. When we moved, some time in the future, I intended to leave my oriole feeder for the new owners with a note saying, "The orioles come with the house."

While I filled my senses with springtime, Bear did introduce a new form of Journey: traveling together out and away from the everyday world. Our first months of conversations had given me time to get to know Bear in the communication style that was my home base: words. But now that our partnership rested on a firmer footing—from all that talking!—I could recognize the feel of Bear's warm support anywhere, and so Bear was ready to begin showing me other places. With one caveat: "The focus on other worlds, as we've said before," Bear said, "is for helping the here and now. Not to say what anyone else's work is, but that's what your work is—for helping the here and now."

The important thing, always, was to let my Helper take the lead. Chris often emphasized how crucial it is to stay close to the Helper's side. "You wouldn't plan a trip through the Amazon without hiring a guide, would you?" she asked. The implication was clear: the less tangible realms are likewise jungles. Staying close to the Helper's side would prevent mishaps because the Helper would protect one firmly from every danger. It was yet another way I didn't have to do all the work myself.

In our first "going somewhere" Journey, Bear merely showed me the inside of a glass door with a metal push bar, the kind found in office buildings. I was invited to push the door open and step outside, where I found a sunny, pleasant sidewalk lined with huge shade trees. What was important, Bear said—in Journeys, apparently, as in life—was simply "the process of going outside and learning from a wider world."

Puzzled, I said, "I thought that traveling somewhere with a Spirit Helper meant going down into the ground or up into the sky or something."

"Stay simpler than that," Bear advised. The cosmology of Lower World, Middle World, and Upper World taught by others, along with directions for traveling to each location, didn't interest Bear in the least. He discouraged me from trying to draw any such mental maps. "Keep the focus in the heart," he said, "in the doing, in the receiving, in the conversation. The reconciling, the communion—that is the thing. The systematized cosmology is not the thing."

Reconciling was an idea Bear had introduced a few days earlier. "Reconciliation is the thread tying together being at home in the self and being at home in the Earth," he had said then. "Reconciliation needs to happen throughout the world—between humans and nature, between humans and the less visible worlds, and within a person." I thought Bear was referring to healing old wounds, but when I tried to say this, Bear pointed instead to his word. "*Reconciling.* Bringing two things into communion with each other again. 'Healing old wounds' can be interpreted as within the self only. And what we're talking about here has to do with *relations*."

Now, after our first very brief traveling Journey, Bear said, "A Journey is always for the purpose of bringing something back to this world—something to give out, to solidify a person's identity so that the person, whether self or another, can exercise their contribution, can put it into play in the world." He clarified by repeating: "Journeying is for the purpose of reconciliation—reconciling with the deep self, with nature, with the less visible worlds." He added, for emphasis, "It's always about right relations."

I found it interesting that Bear did not talk about oneness, as many spiritual teachers do. According to Bear, this path was not about realizing oneness or holding oneness as a goal or seeing one-ness as the true reality behind all apparent differences. Instead, it was about bringing two things back together—healing rifts, bridg-ing chasms, bringing into harmony two things that had worked at cross purposes. Recreating a coherent flow. Overcoming separate-ness. Restoring side-by-side motion. For Bear it was always about relationship. On this path there were always two (or more), and the goal was always partnership.

Bear modeled that partnership with me, for our relationship was intended to be a collaboration. Though Bear, who dwelled in unseen worlds, held a much wider frame of reference than I, who lived in a more limited physical world, and though my life would go much more smoothly if I opened my heart to Bear's larger perspective, this was not a one-way relationship. Bear too needed something. Bear needed a person, a physical person, who wished to be happier and more alive, who wanted to live a more satisfying life. The Helpers would never push their will or their perspective on anyone; it had to be a person's free choice. They truly wanted to be of assistance in this murky world, but their hands were tied, so to speak, until a per-son said yes. Once a person did say yes, then a partnership of strengths could emerge: one person's gift of public speaking or another's accounting skills or yet another's talent for making art could be released, with the support of their own Helper, and brought to fulfillment—its highest good, its most effective purpose. The per-son could feel more at home with themselves, more at home in the world. They could be reconciled.

23

As we began to explore traveling to other locations, Bear invited me to review books on shamanism that I'd read years before, some of which I'd kept on my shelf for decades. In religious studies I had been used to assessing and comparing, so Bear suggested it might be time to clarify my thinking about the way others described this path.

Bear had given me a preface way back in early spring: "This way is *not* about following someone else's pattern," he'd said then. "It's about reaching for what is more simple, more real, more open to the moment. The mental stories get caught up so easily in the head, in how the mind wants things to work out. And that is a different motion from presenting oneself to the moment." It was an odd way of saying it—"the motion of presenting oneself to the moment"— but it perfectly conveyed that stance of being open that seemed to be so helpful in Journeys, and in life.

Now, with the suggestion to review familiar books, Bear continued to encourage an independent spirit. "It is not necessary to accept anyone else's view of how things are," he repeated. Independence of spirit was not merely helpful, it was required on this path, he said. It would act like a motor helping to move the process forward.

With that in mind, I began skimming books. I found that my

experiences with Bear simply didn't match what most of them said. I didn't use drumming to enter a Journey and didn't even own a drum, preferring silence and a quiet mind—and a phone app and earbuds—for talking with Bear. I wondered, Was that okay?

Bear replied with great tact, "Yes, sometimes there is tendency to think that the ways that are taught by others are better. When the greatest gift," Bear added, "is being affirmed in one's own knowing." Though many people might find drumming helpful, Bear suggested that it also had the power to get in the way. "It can remove the immediacy of this conversation," Bear said, "and give people the impression that it's further away from ordinary life than it in fact is."

While many authors had developed techniques for seeking answers to certain kinds of questions, Bear suggested that techniques would only teach me to trust the mind's ability to collect information and to follow others' directions. The real adventure, instead, would be found in trusting my own Helper. Bear recommended that I simply follow his lead, have fun being taken to various kinds of locations, and pay attention to what he wished to show me about each one. The point of my path, in other words, was to cultivate the relationship with my Helper, not to master a body of knowledge. If I wanted knowledge, I could consult written sources, but since I'd already been doing that for years, and since books rarely talked about the warm relationship with a Helper that I was experiencing, they simply were no longer useful.

One idea about animal Helpers that I ran across in books seemed especially different from my experience—the idea that it is necessary for a person to entice their animal Helper to come to them and remain with them, as if they were domesticating a wild creature. In our relationship Bear was modeling the exact opposite: an animal Helper who is always nearby, never leaving, and a human person whose wild heart has to be carefully tamed to stay in that happy, loving presence.

Bear had no interest either in controversies about the terms *shaman* and *shamanic*. If those words communicated something I didn't intend, then Bear advised I find other words. There was nothing sacred about any terminology, including the word *sacred*. "That word is going to be useful in some contexts, less useful in others," Bear said, and then he repeated a by-now-familiar refrain: "What people are yearning for when they look for the sacred is a restored sense of communion. The sense that love and creativity can flow freely. Communion with the deep self, the deep well-springs. Communion with the creativity that keeps the world springing forth with newness." My path was all about communion, he said; it was all about relationship.

24

After having left off mentoring sessions with Chris for some weeks, I resumed them in late May, feeling a need to talk to someone familiar with this process. Chris made it clear that her role was not to be my teacher, in the sense of passing along information. She was instead listening to the Helpers for what I might need at this time, and she would be there to answer questions and support the rich relationship that was developing between Bear and me. "You and I are sitting in a classroom," she said. "You are at one desk, and I am at another. But Bear is at the head of the classroom."

Our first phone meeting was interrupted by a sickening thump at my window. I had heard those thuds before, the sound of a bird crashing into the glass above the back door. It had happened on the first morning we'd lived in this house, and I had rushed to the door, only to spot a raven skimming onto the back deck from out of nowhere and snatching up a small brown songbird where it lay, dazed and still. I didn't want to hear that thump again—or see that raven. I had bought window decals and climbed an extension ladder to stick them onto the glass. The decals may have helped, but every now and again a bird still found a way to collide with the window—one of perhaps a billion birds who crash into glass every year around the world, with an estimated half of them dying from the impact.

On the phone with Chris when I heard the sickening thud, I jumped from my seat, phone in hand, to go help. In my ear I heard Chris calling urgently: "Priscilla! Priscilla! Listen to your guidance!"

I was in no mood to listen to anyone, Helper or otherwise, especially not when I got to the door and discovered it was an oriole who had crashed. On the deck, still as death, lay a yellow-olive bird with a black goatee—a first-year male, likely the one I'd been watching fly among the trees in our yard over the past few weeks in the company of a bright orange mature male, probably his father.

Chris's voice in my ear was disconcerting: What was guidance, anyway? I was a wildlife rehabber; I knew how to handle birds, and I also knew how to rush an injured bird to the local rehab center. Surely the guidance in a medical emergency was to address the emergency, wasn't it?

Feeling confused, I signed off the phone with Chris. Her warning had stopped me just short of charging out the door, picking up the oriole, and placing him in a shoebox with holes poked in it that I kept handy for bird emergencies. Instead I hugged the inside of the door, observing through the glass. From there I could be ready to slip outside if needed to fend off predators.

The oriole lay still. Birds who collide with glass have a head injury and may take fifteen or twenty minutes to recover consciousness. While I watched him I had plenty of time to think. Too much time. Why did Chris's voice hold such a warning? What could possibly be wrong with running out to help the fallen bird?

Feeling confused left me grouchy to boot. I didn't like having my helping instinct questioned. Especially not by my mentor. Surely the urge to help was a good one, wasn't it? If, say, that patio had been a swimming pool, and a child had fallen in, wasn't it my job to help? To call 9-1-1 or dive in if I had the skills for it? This was a life-threatening emergency too, and in this one I actually had the skills to help. Why wasn't I helping?

But as the minutes ticked by and no ravens or hawks arrived to profit from the crash, I started to relax a little and just watch. I tried praying for the oriole—imagining he was lying gently in my cupped hands and allowing warm love and good wishes to flow into me from the Universe and then into him through my hands. Praying for the bird calmed me further. At least I was doing *something*.

It occurred to me that, as twitchy as orioles are about humans, it might actually be better for this oriole to recover by himself. He might be halfway conscious—just enough to panic at the sight of a human and try to flee too soon, perhaps injuring himself further. And what if he came to in the shoebox or in the rehab center? His injured brain would suddenly be flooded with alarming impressions of a cage and entrapment and human lights and human hands. He'd be terrified.

I stood by the door and prayed and wondered about guidance. I was too distraught to hear any—unless the calming down I was doing was one form of it. Most of all I wondered: Was it possible that the urge to help wasn't guidance in every situation? Were there times and places when it was better to do something else, maybe even nothing?

Long minutes passed before the bird lifted his head. It was a full hour before he came to enough to lift himself into the tree branches just above. There he sat for another long while. I could breathe easier now; he had the cover of the tree. His older companion, the bright-orange male, slipped into view. He likely had been sitting nearby the whole time. I began to feel a tiny bit glad that I hadn't alarmed the older guy by rushing out to intervene.

After a very long time the young bird began moving upward in the tree, one slow branch at a time. I left him there, still gathering his wits. In the following days I continued to spot a pair of male orioles, one older and one younger, flying across the yard together. No ill effects from the crash could be seen in the younger bird.

25

The following morning when I sat down for a Journey, I still felt grumpy.

Right away Bear responded in an encouraging voice. "This is not for the sake of confusing you," Bear said. "This is for the sake of finding the biggest definition of compassion. It is easy to get caught up in distress and to want to just fix rather than truly help."

Had I heard right? Was Bear calling out a difference between fixing and helping?

"That's part of it," he said. "This is for making compassion *more* central rather than less. When we are in distress," he explained, "a lot of other things besides compassion can be operating." My urge to help had been mixed up, for instance, with a large dose of alarm. "It's always good to notice what the feeling of distress does," Bear went on. "It makes things very urgent. Sometimes things are not quite so urgent. What Chris called 'staying in touch with guidance' means staying in touch with the purest, warmest heart. You did exactly right, watching to protect from predators," he added. "But watching without causing terror was a *very* good thing to do. Terror is not conducive to healing."

A few days later, when my mind had settled even further, Bear brought up the incident again. On this particular morning he showed up wearing the long, plain work apron of a maid, as starched and proper as a servant in a manor. On a bear it was comical, and on this Bear, who most of the time I experienced as a "he" more than a "she," it was even more incongruous.

Bear, it turned out, wished to offer a little advice about my habit of rolling out of bed at the first hoarse chatter of the orioles, as if I were duty bound to rise with the master's clock and prepare breakfast. Bear observed that it was getting me up sooner than I liked. He was right. Those dawn hours of sleep, when I could get them, were precious.

"Very, very seldom does one need to override the needs of the body," Bear advised. "There are cases, but when the situation is not an emergency, it's a good idea to respect the body's weaknesses." Bear reminded me that when I heard the orioles in the morning, I had a choice. "When people—individuals, humans, birds—are operating with attention to the inner rhythms," he said, "it is not necessary to violate those inner rhythms to take care of others who also have agency and the ability to find what they need."

Ah, now we were getting to the heart of it—that the orioles had agency and an ability to find their own food. I'd been forgetting that. I was regarding them as children who cannot fend for themselves. Bear pointed to my analogy from the window crash a few days before, of a drowning child. My distress—and therefore my urgency—had stemmed from making an equation that was not quite right: I had felt responsible to intervene as I might have for a child. Bear didn't mind comparing birds with humans; it was the child image that didn't quite fit. In relation to birds, Bear said, "it is more like dealing with other adults. It is better to regard them as full-fledged agents, able to take care of themselves, able to know what's going on." Bear suggested that I "avoid feeling the need to help because of a situation of servitude." The words seemed carefully chosen.

But, I protested, aren't humans wrecking the habitat so that it is becoming harder for birds and other wildlife to be full-fledged agents and find what they need?

"Yes, that is true," Bear responded, "*and* it's never a good idea to operate out of guilt. Guilt is one of those ingredients that can cloud the warm heart rather than clarify it. The warm heart acts out of freedom—a sense of freedom and joy rather than the sense of obligation."

There it was—the word that had been hanging around the edges of our conversation up to now: *obligation*. Once I had spoken it, Bear got up, took off the maid's apron, and smoothed his (or her) fur. "No need to feel the obligation," Bear repeated. "We all act in freedom." And gave me a quick thumbs-up for sticking with this conversation even though it was uncomfortable.

Bear added that what we had just talked about carried over in many ways to working with humans. "Begin from that place of enjoying with no urge to change a thing," Bear repeated from our conversations weeks before. "That is the purest form of giving." If I found myself in a situation of offering assistance, I would do well to regard the person in front of me—like the orioles—as fully rich and capable of finding their own solutions. "All that they need is within them," Bear said. "It's right there. And sometimes all it takes is a little tweak, a little reminder. People blossom with encouragement," he added. "Address the fullness of the person more than the lack."

Bear had one last piece of advice: "Keep focusing attention on the Helper, to see what is needed at any given moment. As with the oriole, you may know what to do, and the help may not be needed."

26

At dinner with Tim a few nights later I said, only half joking, "I thought this shamanic training would have to do with, you know, seeing some weird and wonderful things. I wanted to learn about how things work, and I wanted to watch.

"It's not about that at all!" I said. "Instead, it's all about remaking. From the inside out. It's all about changing *me*!"

27

If the path was remaking me, the path was also giving me large doses of reassurance along the way. By early June Bear was encouraging me again to trust my own impressions. Well trained in academia, I tended to qualify my view with the disclaimer that this was just my own lens, my own way of seeing. Bear suggested a slightly different framing. Yes, what I see—what any person sees—comes from a single perspective, but that does not make it any less valid.

Bear recommended "seeing things as they are." I hoped he wasn't talking about trying to see what is true for everyone everywhere. No, he said, this was not at all like that, "not like seeing from a God's-eye perspective." I knew where the God's-eye view led. Every time humans tried to seize the center of reality for themselves or their side, they only ended up coercing others into doing their own will, like the Imperial Stormtroopers of *Star Wars* in their rigid white armor and blaster rifles. "The alternative to the universal perspective," Bear said, "is seeing things as they are. It's much simpler, much closer to home." It's a matter of seeing things *right here*, he said. *Right now.* In one's own environs.

Bear pointed out that this simple practice of carrying on a conversation with a Helper was allowing me to, as he said, "come home to your own deepest, sweetest, quietest realizations. And there is great healing in that. In the past," he went on, "you have been timid about trusting these realizations that were in fact truthful."

He was right. I'd spent years learning to be skeptical of anyone's perceptions, including my own—learning how an outlook can be influenced by a person's surroundings, by psychological wounds, by historical context. Bear framed those years in a positive way; he said they were years of "learning mental balance." I'd done the due diligence, he said, and now I could feel free to reap the reward for all that hard work. "*Now*," he said, "it is time to trust what you have been seeing and have not been quite sure you could trust. You don't have to see yourself as lost in a maelstrom of your own perceptions," he added. "Trust the impressions that are coming to you. They are valid."

I told Bear that, as usual, my mind was doing all kinds of antics with his words. "I don't believe it even as I am speaking it," I said.

"You will," Bear replied.

28

Soon Bear introduced a new metaphor. Up to now we'd talked about the state of mind that stays in touch with love and joy and creativity as a spacious place, a feeling of enjoying with no urge to change a thing. Now he began using metaphors of rivers and currents and flows.

He suggested I try being aware of the currents that flow between all creatures—how every creature makes tracks or currents, not just on the ground but all around themselves through the air, and it is their current or track that defines them. For instance, a male hummingbird doing his mating dance climbs up high into the sky and then plummets to earth, pulling out from the dive at the last second, while an interested female watches from a nearby bush or tree. Bear suggested that what the female is seeing is the whole track, the whole pattern of the male's dive. To her, the complete shape he makes in the sky is "him," not just the physical molecules of his body.

On more than one occasion Bear reminded me to walk in the woods with a feeling of joy and peacefulness in order to leave the best kinds of currents in my wake. Especially if I were to meet a bear, I should remember that enjoyment is a priority for Bear. While caution is always recommended—bears are not to be trifled with—walking in the right spirit can help to keep the peace. "Hunger, yes—it's always good to be wary," Bear said. "But walk in a spirit of joy rather than a spirit of fear, and it will be more in harmony with the surroundings and therefore will have a less disturbing effect on other creatures." Bear repeated, "Walk as an embodiment of that deep joy. That way the currents you make are not distressing or disturbing to others."

A few days later Bear developed the theme of currents in a different way. He reminded me that I was feeling annoyed at a friend who had shown up for our get-together in an irritable mood. What did *she* have to be irritable about anyway? I felt no patience. I said nothing to her, but inside I was rolling my eyes.

Bear showed me a picture of an abstract cube coming out of my head—large and sharp cornered. This was the mental state of being annoyed at or critical of someone. I'd told Tim how irked I felt with this friend, and Bear said that speaking it had allowed it to become more real, to pass outside my own mind and into the world.

"But," Bear suggested, "the point is not just to refrain from speaking those annoyances while keeping those cubes in the head. Much better," he said, chuckling, "is to dissolve those cubes. Liquidate them."

"Can I just say something here?" I asked. "On the surface this conversation is moving along nicely, but underneath I feel totally skeptical of everything—what you're saying, the conversation itself."

"Just keep going," Bear advised. He went on. "Now what happens if you try to navigate with those cubes?" The picture I saw was of a cube-shaped boat trying to move down a wide flat river. It was impossible, of course. Instead of acting like a boat, the cube tumbled and rolled like a boulder, even on the smoothest of currents. It was not a safe conveyance.

"Those sharp mental constructs cannot carry you safely in the current of life," Bear said. "They fight with the current. A negative feeling about someone, either yourself or another, or a critical or judgmental idea or a feeling of impatience—they all impede one's ability to flow down the river. When a person's head is full of a cube of judgment, they can't float serenely. They lose that sense of ease and well-being and fullness in life."

To move easily, Bear said, I needed a boat shaped like the current, like a kayak or canoe. Simply stopping short of thinking critical thoughts would help me swap that cube for a canoe. The job was really about increasing a sense of love. "The more loving conveyance smooths one's way through the current," he said.

"How can I keep from forming those cubes in my head in the first place?" I asked.

Bear suggested that if I notice one forming, to refrain from voicing it. "Words help it become more rigid, more real," he repeated. The rest would be accomplished with time—by learning to know the river, by staying close to the Helper. "As the flow of love becomes larger," he said, "those judgments arise less and less."

And then he sent a feeling of being enfolded in the current, completely held, able to float with ease. It was a feeling of great buoyancy and deep support. It persisted for many hours. People call it "being in the flow," but on that day, instead of just feeling lucky to enjoy it, I noticed how it worked. If an annoyance arose in my mind,

I switched it off, and the feeling of buoyancy continued. Laundry happened with ease. The daily routines of life took place within a great and abiding calm.

But more than that, I felt my awareness grow sharper, clearer. It was not blissful, if *bliss* means an out-of-this-world ecstatic feeling. It was instead ordinary, just a quiet confidence. But it was a place I was not used to dwelling. I was suddenly more aware than usual of plants and trees and animals—not the things themselves but the flows they create. Each one making its own currents, flowing through the currents created by others. Birds flying in paths that respond to other birds, to breezes, to trees, to humans. The everyday world filled with invisible rivers, flows upon flows, every plant and bee and grasshopper and fox and bird and tree giving off its unique pattern and making currents as it moves, and each of them moving in response to all the others and maneuvering around each other's currents and feeling connected to one another through the flows that everyone can see, everyone except us, the humans, who most of the time do not feel those currents and do not respond to the paths that others are creating.

When I was in the flow I was aware of the others and also aware of their awareness—that *they* are aware of *us*, and that this shared awareness makes up the very heart of the flows and gives them their meaning and their life. In the flow I was participating alongside every other creature, and the feeling that arose by being aware of it was a feeling of great affection and deep love, and also a light playfulness, for the flows are a dance, and to become aware of the dance is to enter it with an easy and playful heart. For some hours I played in the dance, enfolded by its fullness, feeling buoyed and supported by its strong currents, able to participate and see and enjoy.

It was a big contrast to the everyday idea that I and most people in modern society live with—that everything other-than-human is opaque to human knowing. "When one gets in the loving flow, the opacity dissolves," Bear commented. "One is simply there. Participating. Responding. Sometimes jockeying. Creating. Being created."

29

The next day Bear suggested I put into words what I had experienced while in the flow, and when I'd described it as fully as I could, he invited me to reflect a little more on the process of writing itself.

I was all ears. So we were going to talk about writing again?

"Writing from within this open connection," Bear explained. "Writing from this feeling of having invited the Helper in to the conversation. This is just a refinement," he added reassuringly. "What needed to be refined, for you, was the idea that writing was the identity."

I didn't understand.

"The idea that writing was the primary activity," Bear explained. The true primary activity for me, he said, is to become more aware of the currents and more deeply immersed in them. "The more fully you are borne along by those currents of awareness," he went on, "the clearer will you know the kind of writing that is yours to do in the world."

As if this interruption in the writing was intended to serve the writing itself! I chuckled, suddenly getting it.

"The writing is not lost, but it needed to be redirected," Bear added, "toward the writing that is the best kind *for you*. And therefore the biggest gift."

As usual, I listened, I spoke what I heard, I transcribed what I had spoken, and then for several years I completely forgot Bear had ever said anything like this.

30

In mid-June we received notice to move. The buyers were under contract with their own house, and they would close on ours on August 1. We had to be out in six weeks.

Panic threatened to rise. I quelled it by going through the list of cities I'd visited over the past year, checking in with Bear for a "getting warmer" or "getting colder" feel on each of them. The consultation was inconclusive. Bear kept saying, "Come to neutral."

I was having a hard time doing that.

Bear said, "It's very important to practice now, when the emotions are higher. Get used to feeling what it's like to drop into the presence of the Helper when the temptation to go off into panic is higher." He suggested that I grasp this relationship as a baby would a pacifier: "something firm to hold on to."

I chuckled. "Bear, I wouldn't exactly describe this relationship as 'firm'!"

Bear laughed loudly. "And you think a house that can burn is firm? Or possessions that can be stolen are firm? What is firmer than your own ability to perceive?"

I was startled—the thing that I'd regarded as most slippery and mutable was in fact the firmest, the most trustworthy?

In the gentlest possible tone, Bear raised a question about all those alternate cities. "The urge to look farther away is the urge to be saved from certain discomforts," Bear said. "Like, not knowing what to do in life. Moving elsewhere will not change that; the question will follow."

Bear did have one suggestion for house-hunting: "Where your spirit goes 'ahhhhhhhhh': dwell there."

It seemed to be advice for mind as well as body.

31

I began house-hunting in Boulder in earnest. I followed ads and spread the word to friends. Every lead came to nothing. It soon became abundantly clear that we simply couldn't afford living in this town. In our six and a half years here, housing costs had skyrocketed so that the kind of house we'd rented at the start now went for half again as much. Our current occupancy had begun as a temporary house-sit, and from all my looking at available rentals, I gained only one horrifying reality check: the rent we were paying now was about half of market value.

How could we possibly find a place where the spirit went "ahhhhhhhh" when my best sources of income had dried up because of this spiritual path and Tim seemed no closer to finding his own niche?

In response Bear said, "Come to the neutral mind! Come to joy!" It sounded like they were the same thing.

I tried to take his advice.

"One gains confidence in the subtler perceptions as one goes along," Bear said. "And a *big* jump can happen by trusting those subtler perceptions even in the middle of outward urgencies—big issues like moving, like illness, like accidents, or like natural—"

I was going to say "natural disasters," but Bear wanted a different term: "overwhelming natural occurrences."

Bear explained: "Those are times of rapid, even overnight, transformations. Your life shifts from one place to another place. And when the outer world is overwhelming in those big ways, it becomes much harder to listen for the still small voice of the Helper, the stiller, smaller, quieter perceptions. But," Bear said with emphasis, "*practice staying attuned to the quieter perceptions. Rest your confidence there.* Don't let those quieter perceptions get obliterated by the massive outer occurrences."

Bear liked the word *occurrences* better than *disasters* because it was neutral, purely descriptive. It didn't obscure an event with a label, determining forever how that event would be thought of. Big occurrences were just things that happen, things that need to happen, in the sense that sometimes big sweeping changes take place that are not aimed at anyone. "So this move is just one of those things that happens," Bear said. "It will take you to the next step. It is the next piece of the journey. Just take it as it comes. Remain attuned to the quieter wisdom." If I could learn to trust that quieter wisdom, Bear said, it would allow me to move more easily. "The quality of motion is cleaner, sharper, crisper, with fewer complications, when one pays attention to the subtler perceptions."

Then Bear invited me to bring to the surface any subtler perceptions I might have about this upcoming move.

I thought for a moment. "One that occurs to me is that we won't actually have to move on August 1." I was hoping we wouldn't because we'd already made travel plans, and changing them would mean enormous headaches.

Bear affirmed that this feeling was accurate, and he encouraged me to bring forward any others so we could look at them together.

"And this contract seems kind of muddy," I said, "so it might not come through, and we might not move in the near future at all."

Bear nodded thoughtfully. "Keep that one in mind," he said. "Keep watching as you go along."

He encouraged me from now on to bring forward all fleeting thoughts, every one of them, so I could consider them in his presence and receive feedback. Perceptions that had merit I could then root myself in, allowing them to take up as much space in my mind as the overwhelming impressions of the outer world.

Then he added, almost as an aside, "That's what guidance is, after all," answering my question from a month before when the oriole had crashed into the window. "Bringing forward those quieter perceptions. Allowing one's reactions to the immediate situation to be tempered, shaped, by those subtler perceptions.

"That's how one stays in touch with the deep joy," Bear continued. And then he broke into a happy dance, an all-out crazy jig, arms up, arms down, kicking feet, turning around. "The quick way to stay in touch with the subtler perceptions," he said, jigging, "is to stay where your spirit goes 'ahhhhhhhh.' The best choices come from this happy place!"

Feeling encouraged to bring them all to the surface, I added one more: "So I get this sense that our next place is in the process of being readied, but it's not quite present yet, so not to spend a lot of time—"

"—going into antics!" Bear interrupted me, laughing heartily. "Not to go into antics over searching for the next place yet, because all the searching in the world won't turn it up until it's ready to be shown."

32

I wish I could say that I followed Bear's advice—that I allowed my mind to settle to a more peaceful place while we waited for the next house to show up. But that doesn't seem to be my way. Though, as Bear said, I was "sinking into the conversation a little more" and "my ability to believe it was growing," I couldn't quite have the confidence of it. I simply wasn't there yet.

So when I petitioned the owners of our house for a later closing date to allow us to complete our trip, and when the buyers said no because *their* buyer was in a hurry and had to have everything done *right now*, I didn't simply rest in the quiet knowing that Bear had affirmed—that we wouldn't have to move on August 1. Instead, I fussed. I fumed. I grumbled. I felt pushed around. I was tired of being at the mercy of other people's schedules. This was the third rental in Boulder—out of four—that we'd been asked to leave because the owners wanted to sell or occupy. It had meant a lot of moving in six years.

When I sat down with Bear, I was feeling very far away from a neutral or joyful mind. I wondered how to temper my reactions so they wouldn't feel so painful.

"Not to toss out a reaction just because it's a reaction," Bear said to my surprise. Then he added something even more surprising. "Stay in touch with the kernel of truth." Often, he explained, reactions of anger or disappointment enclose a piece of accurate perception. The trick is to look closely at a reaction to find the truthful fragment hiding within it. "Stay close to the kernel," Bear said. "Then monitor the reaction. Minimize the reaction as much as possible to minimize suffering."

But even the intensity of the reaction might have a truthful aspect to it, Bear added; it might indicate the extent of the change required or the degree of wrongness present in a situation. "Stay close to the truthful kernel in order to experience the least amount of suffering."

What was the truthful kernel here? In part, that we were feeling vulnerable from all the recent moves, from our shaky finances, from this lingering period of not knowing.

Bear said in a lilting way, "It would be easy to go crazy, being asked to do this much. If you're not going crazy, you're doing okay!"

I almost laughed.

He encouraged me to go ahead with our travel plans as scheduled—a reunion in Oregon, then several days of book readings, with Tim coming along at last for company on a book tour. "It's a little bumpy now," Bear said, "but on the other side of the bumps—oh, so happy!

"This is a universe that enjoys the new, the unfolding," Bear went on. "The unfolding requires shifting. The shifts will reverberate. Don't be too concerned with the shifts. Keep your eyes on enjoying the mystery." This was accompanied by a feeling of peace, as if I were standing and looking out toward hazy blue-lavender mountains, watching the sun rise over their soft, rounded forms. "Stay close to that sense of possibility," Bear advised.

In days to come those bluish mountains would appear in Journeys more than once. I stared hard at them, especially the line of four tiny hills in one stretch of the scene. I wondered where those four hills could be found. If the sun was rising behind them, it had to mean up in the mountains somewhere, since Boulder sat at the eastern edge of the Rockies where the sun always set, not rose, behind hills. Whenever I drove into the mountains I looked east, searching always for that row of four tiny hills.

33

Within days the buyer who was in such a hurry to close the deal with our buyers just as hurriedly disappeared, and our moving deadline was off. We would not have to vacate on August 1, just as Bear had said. I felt I was needing to drop another layer of skepticism about this whole Bear thing.

Right then Bear began talking about where this path I was following might lead in the future. Making the wisdom of the Helpers available to other people was always a possibility, he said, though it depended on if I enjoyed this process of Journeying and if I wanted to do more of it. My answer to both questions was yes, so Bear began helping me think through how it might look. For several days he talked me through possible scenarios—the practical, business side of things as well as the whys and wherefores. He offered advice for both.

But I was still all too aware of my skepticism. How could I know that on this path I wasn't getting goofy?

Bear suggested I look at the particular flavor of my skepticism, and he went ahead and named it for me: "Doubting your listening." He said I didn't have confidence that I was hearing well or that what

I was hearing had validity. "Be aware of the remedy for doubting one's own listening," Bear said. Then he paused.

Okay, I'll bite, I thought. "So what is the remedy for doubting one's own listening?"

"More listening!" Bear said, laughing uproariously. Then he sobered, but only a little: "Coming back to neutral, setting a clear intention of opening to the Helper's guidance." Staying in touch with the body would help, as would settling my feet on the ground a little more deeply. In these ways, and especially through our conversations, I could stay close to the Helper.

Still I wondered: How could I know that what I was hearing was accurate? There were so many ways to *not* hear or see accurately—people predicting things that didn't come to pass; people claiming to see into other realms when you could practically see the hogwash pouring from their mouths; sincere people simply going off-kilter. What did Bear have to say about all those ways a person could run off the rails?

"They fall under the category of Trying to Do It All on Your Own," Bear replied. "Just keep focused on *our* relationship, and you'll see everything you need to see."

Then Bear turned psychologist. He pointed out that doubt in oneself as an adult is created when, as a child, one's unique way of being is tamped down by parents or other adults. "Each child, each person, is due a deep respect," Bear said, "because they have their own purpose." Yet parents or adults may think they have to curb the child's impulses or stop their momentum—actions born of anxiety, of not trusting nature and especially not the child's nature.

"What you experienced as a child was not having your own purposes respected the way they should have been," Bear said. But he quickly went on, "How widespread that pattern is! It has created a deep wound in so very many people! If it happens that a child is not acknowledged at a deep level, she will feel doubt about who she is and what she can do in the world." It is an enormous power wielded by the child's community, Bear said, to shape what an individual considers possible in life.

And because so many people carry this community wound into their adult lives, a community remedy might be called for. Bear began talking to me of the power of a group of people to undo that disrespect and provide instead a place where people can find their individual purposes honored and treasured. Any group, he said, but especially a spiritual group, "is for the sake of releasing the light of the people who come." Bear said it emphatically. "What is *so* desperately needed is for each person to be empowered through their own connection with nature and with the Helpers. There is so much work to be done!"

I felt inspired by Bear's vision for community and began to catch sight of a mission that might unfold further down the road. It was a relief to glimpse even these faint and fuzzy contours of a possible future. Yet the personal implication of his words escaped me at the time. If my doubts about my ability to hear accurately had their origin in self-doubt, it meant that they were not entirely trustworthy; they were a little skewed. Therefore the remedy was to take them less, not more, seriously.

As Bear had said, the remedy was indeed more listening.

34

Once Tim and I had been initiated into the idea of moving, I was ready for it to happen—and right now, please. Enough already with this living in limbo! So in spite of the fact that our place hadn't shown up yet, I began to get the feeling that we would move very soon. Maybe even later in August.

But I wondered: Was I hearing Bear or imposing my own time-table?

Bear responded, in his indirect and respectful way, "When one wishes strongly for something, it's a signal to pay special attention to how the wishing can get in the way." He went on, "You are beginning to feel a great need for the place to move to." He advised that I relax a little more so that I could allow things to unfold. He reminded me of what I already knew: that looking at something with a more open mind—interested, not attached—would allow the guidance to be clear and sharp. Then he brought to mind again the image of the peaceful blue-lavender hills behind which the sun rose, and he suggested gently that I return to what I had been shown and not try to force anything. About that later-in-August date? "Keep checking in because things can change."

I tried to relax and allow things to unfold. I really did. But even I knew I wasn't doing a very good job.

So Bear tried again a few days later. He invited me to reflect on what I already knew about the open, neutral mind. I mentioned the difference between feeling driven to do something and feeling led to do it. "As you know," Bear said, "it is possible that a feeling of being driven is also a feeling of being led. But when one feels driven, it is a better idea to slow down, ask again, and seek the neutral mind." Bear emphasized the quiet, humble quality of the Helper's guidance—not blazing, not blaring, not flashy. Humility was key to hearing that still, small voice.

Joy too would help one find the neutral mind. "You get there much faster through enjoyment than through pressure," Bear said. "That is why we have needed so much attention on enjoyment, because the joyful mind is more in harmony with reality and therefore is by definition a more neutral mind."

It was a startling thought, and this was not the first time Bear had said it. Joy as the neutral place ran counter to every so-called realistic way of seeing things that I had ever heard. Nevertheless, I was beginning to believe Bear's view. Much harder to grasp was his implication: feeling relaxed and joyful about the upcoming changes would help me hear guidance about them more clearly.

As often happened, I didn't take the cue.

35

Meanwhile, the final two book-reading trips that I had arranged in the spring quickly approached. The first, to New Mexico, took place in early July. A few months had passed since I'd done a bookstore reading, and the evening in Albuquerque reminded me why I loved them so much. A peaceful feeling stole around people's shoulders again as they quieted and opened to a story. Hearing about nature connections softened them; it softened me. We could meet in that place we shared, that place of the open heart.

Then it was off to Santa Fe, an hour north, a city I had fallen in love with twenty years earlier, hardly daring to believe in such beauty. Those adobe buildings with blue painted doors—houses of earth with doors of sky! Plus the lilacs—in full bloom during that first visit, their lavender sprays hanging heavy over rusty earthen walls. I'd fallen hard for Santa Fe. I'd visited regularly after that, in every season, thrilling anew to luminarias outlining buildings in December and cottonwood leaves crinkling underfoot in autumn. But the Indian pottery in town was my passion. I stared at pots in shop windows, memorizing their lines, and drew sketches of pots in museums. Then at home I played in clay with those same shapes, learning to make smooth walls on a coiled pot or experimenting with firing in traditional ways with smoke and dung. Santa Fe had become my city of inspiration, my city of dreams.

But a decade had passed since I'd last visited, and many things had changed since then. How would the city look now?

In Santa Fe I stayed with a friend who, when I asked her where I could treat her to dinner, took me to her favorite Afro-Caribbean place, a tiny crowded light-twinkling room called Jambo with the absolute best grilled tilapia I had ever tasted, topped with dried fruit and ginger chutney. Before most book readings I ate lightly, but that night I gorged myself on a full plate, washing it down with tamarind juice. Oh, the joy of it!

The reading went fine, with some thoughtful questions emerging at the end, and the following morning it was time to head for home. I gazed across the adobe buildings downtown, each one settled with time into the crook of the next one's elbow. I still loved the earthen walls, the hint of piñon in the air, the pottery in the windows. But I was different now. More of my home lived inside me.

The realization came quietly, with a small out-breath of relief: I was over Santa Fe.

36

Throughout July Bear talked with me about joy. Every single day. During one Journey Bear might show up in a frilly maid's costume, a reminder to do things I enjoyed rather than things that were imposed by others or by a schedule. Then he would show up in a golfer's hat. (I mean, really, Bear—golfing?) He would circle around a green with exaggerated seriousness, crouching down to line up a putt, standing up again to remove his hat and scratch his head. "The golfers take their activity very seriously," Bear said. "Lighten up! Take it easy, and have fun with this game!"

Another day he might perform a happy, rollicking dance and say, "Get in touch with that feeling of gettin'-down happy! Get on with the day in that spirit." The day after that he might say, "Have more fun! Pay attention to having rip-roaring, belly-laughing fun."

Why all the emphasis on joy? "Joy, love—it's all the same thing," he said. "The flavor that so many people need now is joy. Joy is"— with the picture of a faucet being turned on—"the faucet that turns on the love."

But, I protested, what about all the ways we're destroying the Earth—rushing down a completely wrongheaded path? How can one possibly be joyful in a time like this?

"The way to tackle this crisis," Bear said, "is not the most obvious; it is not what is usually considered first." Yes, he said, energy sources need to be shifted. Yes, we need to quit battering the Earth for fossil fuels. Yes, we need to stop acidifying oceans. Yes, we need to stop torturing whales with sonar and other industrial noises. "*But,*" Bear said, "even given all that, it is good to be willing to tackle the big outer transformations through inner pathways. To tell different stories. To change lives. To approach people through the heart, through story, through imagination.

"Remember mycelium," Bear suggested, the fungus that builds its networks in the damp darkness, growing to become perhaps the largest organism on Earth. "The underground work is powerful work," Bear said. "It will make the biggest and deepest change in the long run.

"As you're finding out," he continued, "there is rarely a sense of urgency. It is not like one can push this river. And so, in one's personal life, adopting an attitude of fun and enjoyment and laughter and lack of urgency may do more healing work than nose-to-the-grindstone hard labor."

He added, "Time is both short and not short. Human actions will have consequences, both short-term and long-term. At the same time, not succumbing to a pressured way of doing things speaks volumes."

37

As July continued into ninety-degree heat and Bear continued to talk about joy, I wondered how to find that place of trusting more deeply in life as it unfolds. In response, Bear opened my question and placed it in a larger arena. He talked about how trusting spirit or the greater wisdom is closely related to other kinds of trust. "Allowing yourself to be carried by this relationship," Bear said, "is allowing yourself to be carried by the processes of nature, the processes of the body, the processes of spirit. These are all facets of the same thing." Conversations with my Helper were meant to support that larger process of trusting what-is. Bear called it "trusting that spirit is implicated in the very foundations of the natural processes; it lies at the heart of them. It is only your society's myopia," he added, "that tends to think otherwise."

"So we have a big joke," I responded, "that someone with a PhD in the worldview of this society rejects the materialist bent—"

"It's more than a bent," Bear interrupted. "The materialist view is the underpinning of this society's whole way of thought." Bear went on, "You're going this way because *nature* led you here. Your evolving relationship with nature. This"—he indicated our conversation—

"is part of nature, though it is not part of the society's thinking about nature."

Bear suggested that the work deeply needed at this time is to heal that divide, the deep belief held in modern society that the physical world is all there is. "Of course," he added, "this is the same as the belief that human beings are not able to know anything other than strictly rational, measurable quantities, that they do not have access to a larger wisdom, no matter how much they have cleared out their own impediments or how well they are listening or have opened themselves." Bear sent a searching glance my way. "As you know," he said, "this is a very difficult belief to overcome, for you encounter the various layers of it in yourself."

It was true. If holding to a radical trust in my own perception seemed daunting, it was but the tip of an iceberg of deeper doubts that, whichever direction I steered my ship, seemed always to be looming straight ahead. My unease with this protracted moving process represented just another layer of those deeper doubts.

"Radical trust," Bear said. "It helps to heal the division between nature and spirit, between self and spirit. Radical trust in oneself, radical trust in nature, radical trust in spirit. All moving about the same center.

"Remember," he repeated, "spirit lies at the *heart* of nature." His eyes were twinkling, to make sure I got the pun. "Staying in touch with the heart is a sure path toward spirit, rather than letting the attention come only from the mind.

"There is a great wisdom," Bear added, "in the joining of mind and heart."

38

The very next day after Bear talked about radical trust, I felt the need to bring up my doubts. "I mean, I don't even really believe this conversation!" I told him.

I felt other kinds of resistance too—qualms about the role this conversation process might be preparing me for. "I'd rather do something more recognizable in the world. I'd rather fit in," I said. I'd been trying to do that all my life, working my way through the acceptable puzzle pieces—musician, editor, writing coach, professor, activist, author, speaker. The problem was that while each of these roles fit what I and other people could recognize, each of them almost but didn't quite fit me. Each piece required a little trimming of the corners. "So here I am, following a process I don't even believe in!"

"Just keep testing everything in your own experience," Bear replied. "There is no need to give assent to something in the mind only. That is blind faith. Test this relationship, and see if it works. Look for results!"

Then Bear offered what sounded like a koan: "Proceeding humbly in radical trust of one's own deepest seeing."

I repeated it slowly: "Proceeding humbly in radical trust of one's own deepest seeing." I recalled how my people, and especially my parents, had seemed to think that "proceeding humbly," which they regarded as all-important, meant doubting oneself—as if it were morally superior to disbelieve one's own perception. For anyone who begins there, the only alternative is to place more trust in the perceptions of others—in holy texts, in civil or church authorities, in the opinions of the community. I came from generations of people who believed the words of others over their own.

My people were hardly alone in this habit. Following teachers and gurus and books and step-by-step instructions laid out by others seemed to be the usual way of going about a spiritual quest. But so many of those teachers and texts pointed only to themselves, not to something larger, and especially not to the something larger that the seeker could find by going within themselves.

"Humility has nothing to do with self-doubt," Bear went on.

I paused. Had I heard right?

"Humility has nothing to do with self-doubt," Bear repeated. "Humility is merely an openness to learning more."

"Okay," I said, still tentative, "suppose this process *is* real. Look, I was educated in the materialist worldview! It takes me a while to unlearn all those layers!" I tried coming to a more open frame of mind. "Do you have anything more to show me about how to come closer to trust?"

"Warm enjoyment!" Bear replied. "Ebullient good enjoyment. Stay in touch with that as you feel your way along."

Of course.

He added, "Practice being carried by this relationship. Spend the day checking out this connection and seeing how life goes when you acknowledge it consciously. If life is better"—there was a big jolly feeling from Bear—"if life is better, well, follow it!"

A few days later Bear returned to the theme. He said, "If this process provides a sense of companionship, if it provides a sense of pleasure, if it provides a sense of purpose or confidence, then follow it out of loyalty to one's own experience." Fidelity to oneself was paramount. "Stay close to the things that provide those qualities of life," he said, "enjoyment, confidence, purpose. Stay close to them out of loyalty to oneself."

I needed the reminder because a friend I'd been close to for many years—the one I'd called from the Santa Monica beach six months earlier at the start of this journey—was uncomfortable with the path I was following, which completely baffled me because for twenty-five years spirituality and meditation had been one of the glues holding us together.

Bear was very direct this time: "Who cares what someone else thinks about this process? Who cares if one's best friends question it? They are following paths that give *them* pleasure and purpose and meaning. Plant oneself firmly in loyalty to one's own experience."

He said that this was a stumbling block for many people— becoming willing to give up their own fullest life because it might not find approval with others. "They relinquish that loyalty to themselves," he said, "in favor of what someone else might think, in favor of not looking stupid or not looking gullible or not looking wacky. But no one but the self can nourish one's own deep streams," Bear went on. "Do not relinquish them to someone else's opinion." He recommended what he called "radical loyalty to the self. Radical loyalty to what works in one's own experience."

39

My second trip in July, and the round of bookstore readings and classroom visits that would complete the first year of the book's life, led us to Oregon. We spent a sun-drenched weekend in the southern forests of the state to celebrate a niece's wedding and then headed north, enjoying on the way a side trip to the coast, which was socked in during the final days of July with a cool and quiet fog.

In one university town where I was scheduled to do a reading, we'd failed to find friends to stay with and ended up in grad student shared housing—an enormous, two-story mansion within walking distance of campus. We picked our way through its tiny, tangled yard, entered the huge front door, and headed up the front staircase. Its carpet was threadbare and ratty, the room at the top small but high-ceilinged. In it we found a single bed. Had I forgotten to warn them that Tim was coming with me?

Our dissertation-writing host was friendly and gracious as he could be, and when he met Tim he immediately mounted the ladder to the attic, dragged down a second single mattress and box spring, and set them up for us catty-cornered because the room was too small to hold two beds side by side. He scrounged up sheets and pillowcases and a towel for each of us. The showers, we found, were dorm-style with creaky three-quarter doors that barely latched and no shelves inside for toiletries. Above the row of bathroom sinks was taped a note hand printed on a 3x5 card: "Others live here too. Wipe out your own sink. —The Housekeeper." The once-plush charcoal carpet in the hallway looked as if decades ago it might have started out as emerald green.

But every time we entered the kitchen—an enormous, high-ceilinged room with an industrial sink and stove—we found one or another of the doctoral students fixing a sandwich or chopping vegetables around the room-size center island. We would introduce ourselves and get caught up immediately in a lively conversation, laughing and talking and discovering that we knew the same people. While Tim and I ate dinner on the orange vinyl sofa in the living room, our host sat with us, and we talked of nature writing and social change and philosophy and all the things that had mattered most to me in an earlier academic life. I left that town with a list of new friends.

40

Back home in August, I offered a workshop to keep myself busy, but what I was really doing was waiting on pins and needles for our next house to show up. Would it perch on the side of a mountain, where I could watch the sun rise over those blue-lavender eastern hills? I was ready for that kind of solitude, being surrounded by nature. Or would it sit at the edge of town—easier to get to if I offered more workshops? Most of all I wondered how in the world this miracle would happen. I was beginning to believe it was possible, but not enough to settle myself quietly in the knowing. From time to time we'd hear of a new lead on a house, but each one soon evaporated to nothing.

Bear, meanwhile, began showing up for our conversations in the most nonchalant manner I'd seen yet. One day he might be sitting contentedly in a rocking chair, eyes shaded by a straw hat, dozing. The next he'd be lounging on a chaise in sunglasses, paws clasped behind his head. "Another day off!" he'd announce, grinning. He called it our "August demeanor," laughing heartily at his own joke. Now, several years later, I can see the invitation—to pull up a virtual lounger myself and just sit and enjoy some vacation time with Bear, to relish the present moment with no urge to change a thing. But at a time when I was itching to get on with things, being told there was nothing to do and nowhere to go did not strike me as good news.

"Take it easy, and keep enjoying!" Bear said.

I tried to keep from rolling my eyes.

41

I mused about how putting a personal face on spirit had been a stretch for me in the past.

"*Is* a stretch for you," Bear corrected. "Let's keep it in the present tense."

I'd grown up being taught to pray to Jesus and later had explored Tibetan and feminist goddesses. Yet conjuring up the image of any sort of spiritual figure had always worn thin after a while. I thought I'd left that path of personality long before.

As a graduate student I'd come to rest in a skeptical or agnostic view, and even in theological school I'd had plenty of company. Many of us religion students hung around the edges of faith, enjoying the bells and smells of religious rituals, appreciating hints of another world, loving the warmth of community in churches or synagogues or sanghas yet feeling just a hair—or maybe a lot—more comfortable documenting and discussing and comparing those traditions than actually practicing them. Though we respected the life of the heart, we chose the light of human reason. Any possible reality outside the physical senses we regarded as murky, impervious to human knowing.

There was a certain convenience to being an agnostic. It was intellectually respectable, for one thing. It didn't require departing from scientific materialism, the model guiding intellectual life in the modern world. It bestowed the comfort of fitting in.

But now I had to notice something else. In spite of the fact that this path violated what I tended to think of as possible—and definitely, hoo-boy, what I thought of as respectable—it was completely consistent with what I'd written a book about: developing deeper relationships with nature, listening to other voices, opening our human perspective to more-than-human wisdom. The friend who had laughed and said, "You mean you didn't know?" had been exactly right. This path fit. It was a lot more consonant with who I was than I'd had the grace to admit.

Around the middle of August Bear suggested I put into words a little shift I was feeling.

"Before," I said, "this path felt a little foreign, and I was testing it and fearing I wasn't doing it right. But now—"

"Acceptance," Bear interrupted. "The inner acceptance."

"Yes," I said. It wasn't yet complete, but I was taking another step. The wary watcher inside was relaxing just a trifle. "This way of relating *is* enriching," I said. "It's *my* path." More and more I was finding myself able to just pull up a rocking chair beside Bear and enjoy. "And I'm having more fun!" I added.

"*Another* day off!" Bear chuckled, eyes twinkling.

42

Suddenly one morning when I sat down and quieted my mind, Bear showed up tugging on my hand. "Come on! Let's go!" There was a sense of anticipation, of looking forward to a new adventure.

We traveled to a spot on the Earth with low scrub all around, like the deserts of the Southwest. The ground was stony, cream colored, bright in the blazing sun.

I looked at Bear. "What about this place?"

"Remember this landscape," Bear said. "Note this scene and file it away."

A couple of days later Bear again invited me to travel. Then he pulled back his lips to bare his enormous teeth. "Remember, I'm the one with the teeth," he said. "I watch out for the safety."

And so the traveling Journeys began in a relaxed and gentle way. We might go to a place I hadn't seen before and simply sit and enjoy the view, chatting amiably. Early on during one of these chats I wondered why Bear had waited two months to begin traveling after he'd introduced the idea.

"It takes a certain calmness in the body before this kind of Journeying becomes stable and accurate," Bear replied. I was going to say "authentic," but the word Bear wanted was *accurate*. "Stable and accurate." Then he invited me to watch the sun rise in this land I'd never seen before.

When we returned from that Journey I felt a little hazy the rest of the day, not quite present. Bear advised I get used to what it feels like to go on a somewhat deeper Journey and then return to every-day reality.

"The draw toward the traveling world can be so strong, espe-cially for beginners, that it's good to plant the feet firmly in the everyday world," Bear advised. Taking care of daily business, prepar-ing food and eating and cleaning up, hiking with Tim and Bodhi, doing yoga would all help me stay rooted in the everyday world.

More and more often Bear appeared at the opening of a Journey with a paw extended: "Want to come?" All I had to do was grasp that big furry paw or lock wrists and enjoy being shown around. Before meeting Bear I had experimented with going on imaginative journeys, but I'd always felt that I was making them up—which, if I was lucky, I was in fact doing, because going on my own amounted to wandering in the Amazon without a guide.

Traveling with Bear felt different. I had someone to focus on who knew where we were going and who had made sure I was pre-pared in all ways for the trip. If Bear wanted to fly out the window in real time and sit on the ridge of the foothills a half mile away, I could enjoy being shown this new view of my own neighborhood. We might sit close on the ridge, Bear's huge arm around my shoul-ders—safe, peaceful, warm, a feeling of coming home. Or if Bear wanted to travel to a different time or place, I could enjoy going there and exploring alongside him. Each trip, each scene was meant to be nourishing at the same time that it extended my ability to follow Bear into terrain that over the next months grew less and less familiar as it grew further and further removed from everyday experience. Whatever scene we explored, it was not up to me to decide what happened there, for I was being taken on a tour; it was not up to me to figure out why or how, for I had a tour guide.

In between traveling Journeys, Bear was still all about joy. One day he said, while resting his belly on the ground, slightly curled up, head on his front paws as if snoozing, "Love, appreciation, enjoyment, happiness—they are the center of health. They are the foundation of the world, the flowing river itself." He called love "the stuff of which everything is made," the very lifeblood of the world.

"Live from here," Bear said. "This is the place to keep coming back to, moment after moment, day after day." Then he opened one eye enough to wink at me before going back to snoozing.

43

Were the locations Bear showed me "real" locations—traveling "out of body," as many people suggest? Bear didn't pay much attention to these categories, and soon neither did I. Some places I recognized; others I did not. As I grew more adept at following Bear, he might take me somewhere new and then, for fun, ask me where we were, and I'd look around and notice the quality of light or darkness, of motion or stillness—the overall feel of the place. We might be in outer space (the very large) or a blood vessel (the very small), and the only reason it seemed to matter was, for instance, if the blood vessel we were visiting was mine and Bear had something to show me about my own health.

Even in recognizable locations, the Journeys often unfolded in the language of symbols. Visible and metaphorical realities continually flowed in and out of each other, inseparable. In a blood vessel I might see recognizable cells but also metaphorical images of other "lifeblood" activities. Reality in a Journey often behaved differently than in the everyday. The point was not to master "how things look" or "where things are" or "how things behave"—a mental activity aimed at accumulating static, contextless knowledge—but rather to pay attention to *this* place, *this* picture, *this* feeling, and what the Helper was sharing in *this* moment. Bear repeated often that Journeys are intended to be helpful for *this* world. "It's a simple heart-purpose," Bear said. Journeys provide fuel to help people move more smoothly through life, to help them be reconciled.

Most of the time Bear's advice was simply to keep an open mind regarding the places I was being shown. He seemed happiest when I stayed both playful and serious—playful enough to enjoy conspiring in a fun adventure with my Helper while at the same time taking the impressions seriously enough to keep following them and regarding them as worthy of attention. "These travels that we do," Bear said clearly, "have equal importance with the everyday waking world."

At the same time, Bear said that the wisdom offered in a Journey was not exhausted by how it might be applied to the need of the day. Though I could trust that Journeys always had a purpose, that purpose often was not immediately clear. Sometimes, yes, a Journey related directly to things I was experiencing in the everyday world; sometimes it didn't. He advised against taking a pragmatic view of Journeys, reducing them to anything like a daily lesson. Instead, he said, "It is always necessary to give the Journeys a great deal of space, a great deal of room, to be what they want to be and to do what they want to do." If I remained in a lighthearted frame of mind, I could trust that in due time their fully layered richness would emerge.

Often I fell behind in transcribing, and then, when I returned to a Journey two weeks or three months later to type it up, the very thing it talked about would be happening in life at that point. I began to have a sense that every moment in life is watched over— not planned, exactly, not planned at all, in fact, but somehow encouraged forward with great attention and care. As if each person, each creature, were a thread in an unfathomable tapestry, each one carrying its own thread across the fabric, pausing here, detouring there, adding to the design. But instead of becoming chaotic, as you might expect from a tapestry woven by multitudes, the design emerged coherent, beautiful—though you had to take quite a few steps back to appreciate it.

Was I in a trance when I talked with Bear? This question got brushed away with a huge furry paw. It wasn't worth the time it might take to talk about it. Suppose I went to a café to have tea with a friend and got absorbed in the conversation, losing track of time; was I in a trance then? Did it matter? If not, why did it matter when I talked with less-physical friends? All that language of trances and out-of-body experiences, Bear said, makes this process of hanging out with a friend seem exotic or complicated—further removed from ordinary life than it really is. Better to just focus on cultivating the relationship.

Now and then Bear invited me to explore the experience of being various kinds of animals. He said that what humans call empathy, or being able to feel with another, is related to this other ability to actually enter into another's experience. After one Journey that included two or three different animal bodies—fun of course but far removed from the things that I thought at the time were *really* important, like enough income to live on and especially a new place to live—I couldn't resist asking a question: "I wonder, Bear, how to use this. What good is it?"

Bear was ever patient. "Storytellers need it," he replied. "People who mentor others need it. People who wish to delight in the world could do with a good dose of it!"

44

On the last day of August, after Bear had taken me out and away in previous days to a number of unrecognizable places, he returned to exploring the ridgeline above our neighborhood. In Journey we traveled to the top, and I paused to look out—the view of Haystack Mountain to the northeast, the city of Boulder spread out, humming, to the east and south.

But those were not the things that interested Bear. He was instead moving along the ridgeline close to the ground, looking down at the surface of the earth. When I did that too I saw big rocks, a lot of prairie grass in its late-summer garb of golden yellow. But Bear was especially interested in the places where the waters began—each of the hollows where water gathered and flowed down the eastern side of the ridge, each of the canyons hosting a stream that flowed through town. He followed one stream down from the ridge through its channel into the nearby urban lake. His demeanor was quiet and thoughtful. Then he led me back up to the ridge to sit quietly and look out over the lake. We sat and sat. I kept thinking he was going to get up and do something, but he just sat. Bear sat so quietly and for so long, simply gazing out over the land, that I grew bored and impatient, barely able to keep myself by his side.

"Just sit in peacefulness," Bear suggested.

When we returned from the Journey I told Bear, "That wasn't what I was expecting!"

It seemed to be the point—to have patience with the unexpected, to help me build trust in my Helper.

45

In early September a crisis that had been building for some weeks suddenly boiled to the surface. I had been expecting to move by now, and when it didn't happen, I was thrown. My budding faith in the path was shaken, my oh-so-tentative visions of the still-fuzzy future thrown to the wind. I lost all sense of meaning; I couldn't figure out the way forward. I felt miserable.

Day after day Bear patiently heard me out but politely declined to respond. Then just as patiently he would extend a paw—"Want to come?"—and lead me on yet another marvelous if puzzling adventure.

Looking back now, I can see the comedy—my railing against the not-knowing at the very same moment that Bear was quietly, steadily continuing to lead me through one traveling Journey after another.

It took talking the problem through with Chris before I finally understood what had happened. I had thought I'd heard about a September move from my Helper. When it failed to materialize, I lost faith, again, in my ability to hear. All the marvelous Journeys in the world couldn't hold my attention if I was just making them up after all.

But Chris had one question: "Did Bear say September?"

I went back through the transcriptions. No, I guess not. Instead, Bear had offered cautions about how easy it is to lose accuracy in hearing the Helpers when a person is eager for something, wanting it very much. I'd skipped right over those parts. I'd followed my own wishing more than Bear's words. It wasn't a case of hearing inaccurately; it was a case of passing what I'd heard through a filter of intense wanting, of attachment. My mind had run into the future, connecting dots that were just dots. I'd gotten my own fingers in the mix, as Chris liked to say.

I took a deep breath. It was time to come to neutral again.

"Just be willing," Bear advised.

46

The late-summer weekend turned sunny and hot, with the temperature on Sunday, September 8, hitting ninety-three degrees, a new high. To everyone's relief, clouds gathered the following day, and rain began before nightfall. It started slow and tentative. We encouraged it on—maybe we'd get a break from the drought plaguing eastern Colorado. On Tuesday the rain gathered speed, and by Tuesday night it was pounding steadily on the roof. Oh, blessed sound! The rain droned on and on through the night. This would surely refill those sagging reservoirs.

When, on Wednesday, September 11, the rain poured down again all day, even harder than before, we grew uneasy. The ground was saturated, and still the rain kept falling. Standing water appeared on roadways. By Wednesday night we were frightened. The wind had picked up speed, and torrents of rain lashed every house.

The rain that night was unyielding. It pummeled every roof as if demented. Water filled streets and flowed across the paths of cars. It threatened to top reservoirs and crumble dams. Boulder Creek, flowing through downtown and the university, rose to flood stage, then beyond. We sat glued to computer and phone screens, checking news and flash flood warnings. The rain was falling at the rate of three-quarters of an inch per hour. Evacuations at the university started at ten. An hour later two nineteen-year-olds left a birthday party in the mountainous neighborhood a mile above ours and were stranded by water flowing across the street. When the two climbed out of their car to make a dash for it, each of them was swept away. As I went to bed at 1:00 a.m. they still had not been found. (Their bodies were recovered later.)

I woke early on Thursday after broken sleep to still-pounding rain. In the dusky morning light—gray and dim compared to the usual bright morning—I pawed to the back of a closet to find old yellow rain slicker pants and jacket, the foulies I'd bought years ago for sailing on the San Francisco Bay. I pulled them on, tucking my phone into a waterproof pocket, and headed out. I had to get to know this storm.

I didn't have to walk far. At the bottom of our hill, muddy water rushed in a torrent across a major street. The landscape had been reshaped overnight by a tiny creek that usually trickled in a shallow ditch beside the road but now had transformed into a raging river. In one night it had swept enough rocks and mud down from the mountains to fill to level a fifty-yard-wide, fifteen-foot-deep, always-dry overflow pond. It had scoffed at the puny culvert placed in the ditch to carry it off to a different sector of town and instead reclaimed its historic creekbed. The river was now roaring, full and free, down the street and across a neighborhood, following the ancient contours of the land.

I looked down its cross-country path toward the houses standing in its way. They'd been built in the middle of a forgotten creekbed, and I could only imagine the pounding they were taking from this new-old river, a river that remembered where to go. Other neighbors too had come to watch. We milled around the edges of brown water, not believing.

I picked my way carefully over the rock-strewn remains of what used to be a sidewalk up to the street above ours, a street hugging the foothills. There I found an SUV tipped on its side, abandoned, where this new river had obliterated the roadway with its raging flow. On the steep hillside behind the houses I could see tall, skinny gashes ripped into the slope—narrow mudslides one after another slipping down the hill and charging into the houses below. People from one house were walking, dazed, around the unharmed front of their property. The back of their house had turned into a gateway of mud.

And still the rain poured down. Though I took only a few photos, slipping my phone out of my pocket for less than ten seconds at a time, the rain was falling hard enough to short-circuit the phone. It dialed, on its own, the last person I'd talked with the day before.

I hiked out to the hillside above the small urban lake. At its top lay the ridge where Bear had taken me in Journey on the last day of August, where we had looked at the channels of flowing water, where Bear had sat—and sat and sat—gazing out over the lake. The air was gray now with rain, the lake the color of mud. The grassy hillside, which Bodhi and I had watched in every season and every kind of light, wore a face I'd never seen before: it was shining silver. Water continued to pour off it, twinkling in the gray light.

Suddenly I realized I was putting myself in the path of possible mudslides, and I hurried downhill toward home.

The rain pounded all day Thursday. By nightfall, nine inches had fallen in the previous twenty-four hours, smashing all records. The saturated ground could simply hold no more, and it released the waters into every available basement. Sewer lines backed up, filling lower floors with raw sewage. A significant portion of homes in the city flooded—not from overflowing creeks but from waters rising up out of the earth itself.

In communities north and south of Boulder, bridges collapsed, dams burst, roads washed away. Houses were shoved roughly down-hill near every creek that wound through the mountains to the plains. Catastrophic flooding occurred throughout a hundred-mile stretch along the Front Range. It was as if an enormous, silver-gray giant had parked itself like a statue for a week between mountain and plain, one limb resting in each of the canyons up and down this stretch of land. Was it sightless, taking up residence without love or malice for a week and then moving on? Or was it in fact kinder than it might have been, holding back some of its true power out of regard for the people below?

Bear said only, "These forces are *way* more powerful than people are remembering from day to day—forces of water, forces of clouds, weather systems. These forces *will* have their way. And it's a matter of how flexible human beings can be to respect the massiveness of the forces' power."

By the time the rain stopped for good, on Monday, Boulder had received a year's worth of rainfall, seventeen inches, in the space of one week. Then the cleanup began. Piles of debris sprouted for several long weeks at the ends of driveways, and carpet-cleaning vans droned loudly on every street. Rebuilding roads and houses took months longer.

Our house was spared any flooding, one of only two or three on our street with no leaks, which greatly relieved both us and the owners and also greatly reassured the buyers. That any houses at all on our street had filled with water was surprising, for our cul-de-sac traced the side of a hill that in wintertime served as a sledding hill and in summertime saw neighbors gather to watch the fireworks across town. It was one of the highest spots in the city.

But my dandelion-pulling coconspirator filled me in on the history of this hill. In the time before Europeans it was known as a sacred hill because of its naturally flowing springs. Indians did not pitch their tipis on this hill, for it was too sacred, only visiting it for vision quests and ceremonies. When the street was slated for development in the 1970s, the Arapaho who remained in the area objected, to no avail. The developer had named it Wonderland Hill—a small gesture toward its sacred character.

After the flood Wonderland Hill sloughed off its cactus-sprouting modern garb and returned to its older, wetter self. The rains had filled its deepest cisterns to overflowing, and for months afterward, here and there across the hill, water seeped out and trickled downward. Dozens of seeps. Anytime Bodhi and I traced one of the footpaths crisscrossing the hill, we got muddy feet. Ambling around and over the hill on our afternoon walks, I enjoyed thinking about the prayers that had been offered here, the gift of water that had flowed here, the visions for living that had been received on this hill. It was the hill where I'd stayed when I first visited Boulder and fell in love with the area's beauty. It was the hill where Tim and Bodhi and I had lived for five of our six and a half years in town. Wonderland Hill still supported visions; it was still a hill of far-seeing.

For several weeks after the flood I also walked down to the bottom of the hill to watch the newly engorged river continue to flow across the street. So did many of my neighbors. We were making pilgrimages to the water, listening to its messages, trying to wrap our minds around its power.

47

Several weeks after the flood, I joined a naturalist-led hike to see what the storm had done to Chautauqua Park and all its trails lying just below the Flatirons. Most of the group knew these trails like the backs of our hands; we'd hiked them dozens or hundreds of times.

Only a short way into the hike, a new world met us. The trickle of a stream that used to meander down the center of the park and under a stone bridge had swollen during the flood to unrecognizable size. It was still flowing several feet wide. Its narrow creekbed had been gouged into a wide-open canyon. Before, close-set, brush-covered banks had guarded the seasonal trickle, with butterflies and hummingbirds hovering under a tangled canopy of arching trees, but now a broad sandy channel greeted us, scrubbed clean of anything green. The trees were gone; the brush was gone. Only sand and gravel remained, along with gleaming boulders the size of trucks.

Also standing was the bridge, a low hulking thing of stone and concrete built by the Works Progress Administration in the 1930s. Though its upriver facade of decorative stones had peeled off, the bridge itself had stood firm. The naturalist explained that this bridge had actually stopped the largest boulders from flowing downriver onto the streets—and cars and houses—below. From the middle of the bridge, we looked up. Boulders towered over our heads. Down-stream the boulders were half that size. This bridge was being renamed the Hero Bridge in honor of its service during the flood.

The scene farther up the trail astonished us most. In a cordoned-off area we walked upstream to a spot where narrow, overgrown trails on either side of the tiny creek used to be joined by a small footbridge a few feet long. Now the place was unrecognizable. Fifty-foot-deep canyons—two of them, each many feet wide—had been punched side by side into the sloping hill under the Flatirons. Exposed dirt stretched up and down what used to be a tiny stream-bed but was now a deep canyon riverbed as far as the eye could see. We picked our way down boulders to the bottom of the new canyons and looked up, trying to imagine the power that had excavated in a few hours so many tons of earth and rock.

I could almost hear the explosions. On the night of September 11, with rain pouring down, water sheeted off the Flatirons onto the ground below, racing toward the creek. The thousand-foot-tall slabs of red sandstone were impermeable, so all the rain falling on their half-mile stretch of rock gathered on the ground below, soaking in, percolating down, down, down toward the hollow of the creek. Still the rain pounded, and still the water raced, filling the creek to over-flowing, flooding its banks, saturating the ground beside and below the creek, building pressure in the banks of the creek, more and more pressure, more and more water, until with a great groaning, slow at first, then faster and faster, the ground began to release. Picking up speed millisecond by millisecond, with a tremendous shudder the earth tore itself loose from its banks and joined the raging waters. Ripping out boulders as it went, the flood roared down the creekbed with a sound that neighbors later described like that of a freight train. Truck-size boulders dropped at the bridge, but the water rushed on, the once-narrow creekbed many times as wide as anyone had ever seen it, water rising halfway up its steep canyon sides. And still the torrent rushed down, down, finding the street, slamming into cars lining the street and washing them down toward the plain. As the rains continued, the waters would grow, tearing more rocks and dirt out of the hillside, punching those new canyons deeper and wider with every passing hour.

The scope of the changes overwhelmed us. The earth had transformed overnight, and we had been here to watch. Creeks and canyons that we thought were so dependable, so "there," had disappeared, replaced by contours we couldn't yet recognize. The changes that we always imagined taking place over eons in fact took place in explosive moments—in a single day, in two or three days—every century. Geologic changes had been sculpted in a single night.

Now we could understand the enormous boulder, ten feet wide and eight feet tall, that had rested beside a building on the lawns of Chautauqua for as long as anyone could remember. It had been carried there by torrents of water in a previous flood in a time before lawns, a time before buildings, a time perhaps even before time itself.

I returned every week to stare at those brand-new canyons, marveling.

48

After an overwhelming natural occurrence, people always try to figure out why it happened. Some kinds of calculations are helpful, like
digging into historical records to see how an event compares to the
past or measuring a storm against climate change models. When the
weather scientists of Boulder did these calculations, they came to a
startling conclusion. With everyone else talking about how rare this
flood was, how out of proportion to other floods, the meteorologists
called attention to how normal some of the numbers actually were:
any given creek in the area, such as Boulder Creek flowing through
downtown, could be expected to flood to these levels not merely
once in a century but a handful of times. It was up to humans to
plan for and expect such events.

What *was* rare was the square mileage of this storm—spreading
up and down the Front Range, flooding dozens of creeks at once,
and extending all the way into New Mexico. No emergency teams
had been prepared for that. Also rare was the total rainfall, which
flooded areas far away from creeks. Ground flooding in dry Boulder?
It was unheard of. Though scientists claimed at the time that climate change had not contributed to this storm, we all wondered.
(They revised this conclusion two years later when links between

warming oceans and supercharged storms became clearer. There was a good chance the severity of this storm had been increased by global warming.)

If meteorologists were making the helpful kinds of calculations—helpful because they held up a mirror to human acts, a mirror that could be used to guide human choices in the future—people looking for the spiritual meaning of the flood all too often fell back on unhelpful clichés. One of those clichés was the easy metaphor, something one often hears in cases of illness or overwhelming events. After a forest fire, people might say that purification had been necessary, or after a flood that some cleaning-up must have been needed. Those who resort to easy metaphors obviously don't live in the affected areas, for when you find yourself on the butt end of one of them, you suddenly develop a keen ability to hear just how brimming it is with judgment.

"People tend," Bear said, "to look back and think that something was necessary." He didn't care at all for the habit. "The forces of nature are much more objective than that." The flood was a coming together of forces—a communal affair—and finding meaning in a helpful way meant looking in a different place than why it had been necessary or who needed to be taught a lesson. "In the face of forces as large as this one," Bear said, "human ways of putting the pieces together tend to fall short. And they especially fall short when they rush to conclusions about why an event happened, because those conclusions often carry a tone of judgment."

He went on, "There is some confusion in people's minds between a spiritual perspective and a judging perspective. People who jump to what they think is a spiritual perspective," he added, "are not at all getting outside their own limited sight." He recommended against seeking spiritual explanations for events. "Human beings simply are not wise enough to draw those conclusions. Human sight is simply not large enough to see."

Instead of asking why an event was necessary, Bear said a truly spiritual perspective would mean offering encouragement and support. "When we're dealing with forces as mighty as wind and water and clouds," he said, "the more encouraging perspective, the more supportive one, is to deal with the realities rather than speculate on reasons." It was more a matter of holding up the event as a mirror, as scientists had done for the physical view, in order to see what it reflected back to a person about where to go from here. It meant drawing connections between the personal and natural—hints for the future rather than judgments about the past. It meant listening for what the event might make possible, what avenues it might open up. For you.

Bear modeled just this kind of encouragement. In September I continued to feel restless and out of sorts—a feeling of no-place, which of course made sense after months of uncertainty not only about where to live but also about who to be and what to do in life. Would anything at all that I'd learned in the past be useful from this point on?

Bear sounded an exuberant "Yes!" He saw that it wasn't sitting well with me to be a beginner again, and he assured me that nothing would be wasted. "All that you know will be used," he said. But it would be most helpful if I could put all that aside for the moment to focus on what he and I were doing here. "The bigger way of putting it all together in the future requires going around it," Bear said, "like water goes around a dam. It involves finding a new path of least resistance down the hill." I saw again the waters flowing down hillsides, across streets, finding new ways around rocks and other obstacles. "The waters do all come together at the bottom of the hill again," Bear said. "But we're in the process of finding a new way down."

In a session with Chris, Bear had more to say about my discomfort. He shared with her that there was some stubborn part of me that didn't want to let go of feeling disagreeable about this process. In that shadowy recess I was simply closed; I was determined to dislike what the process required and where it was taking me.

The morning after he'd said this I woke up before dawn from a discomfiting dream that ended with these clear words: "your fundamental disquiet with how things are."

When I sat down later that day to talk with Bear about my temper tantrum, he would hear none of it. "Let's call it an identity shift instead," Bear said. My term would magnify it, when in reality it was more like a pesky mosquito that one needs to flick off the arm. "Companion yourself well through this identity shift," Bear said. With a chuckle he added, "It has never been a simple thing for you in particular to change identities."

I told Bear I felt that I'd lost my moorings.

He recommended that I focus instead on a feeling of gain. It was possible—especially if I kept my mind open—that this identity shift would lead toward something bigger and more satisfying than the most satisfying thing I had done yet, namely, writing a book. "Go toward a sense of gain," he repeated.

I would have to dig deep to find it. I thought again of Baba: "Find the sweetness in the bitterness."

Then Bear returned to the images that were never far from any of our minds in those weeks after the flood. "A flood will knock out the roads, but that is only temporary," Bear said. "The roads can be fixed again, and better paths can be found to allow the water to flow more freely." And then, as if to tantalize me with the rich streams to be discovered along this path, he led me on a traveling Journey with the theme of currents and flows that was the most complex and fascinating and fun Journey yet.

I began to see that all the roads I had laid down so carefully to get around in the world, all the structures I'd built to help me find an identity, could interfere with the waters that were right now bursting free.

I prayed to become willing—willing to allow those structures to fall, willing to follow the water where it might flow. I asked that I might keep the ancient water-paths wide open.

49

By the end of September the fields encircling Boulder had drained of their flood moisture, and in my favorite raspberry patch berries hung red and fat on the canes. Mosquitoes buzzed thick over the damp earth, but I threw on a long-sleeved hiking shirt and pants and hoped for the best.

I spent two sun-drenched days plucking ruby-colored jewels under a sapphire sky. Ten or twenty pounds of berries at home meant I could devour raspberries without restraint. A series of digestive challenges in recent years had narrowed the range of foods I could handle, but raspberries continued to provide the gift of gorging freely. Berries always made my belly happy.

During a Journey with Bear after berry picking, I mentioned how much I loved raspberries and was not surprised to hear Bear concur. Of course a bear would love berries! Bear said they were better for me than my favorite fruit, peaches—a comment I completely overlooked until months later when I learned that I had developed a sensitivity to stone fruits (which explained the near-constant headache that August and September during peach season).

Then it occurred to me to ask, Were there other foods that might be especially good right now? Instantly a picture of cheese came to mind. Cheese with big holes in it. Swiss cheese. Especially high-quality, dry aged Swiss.

I protested. "Um, Bear, I've been off dairy for fifteen years. I don't eat cheese." But then it occurred to me to try being more open about this cheese thing. Was there perhaps something about cheese that I was missing?

I shifted mental gears and asked, "What is it about cheese?"

Instantly I saw a picture of a word on my mental screen, a word that I recognized but did not know the definition of or even how to pronounce: c-a-s-e-i-n. Then Bear fell silent, and no more information emerged.

As soon as the Journey finished I opened my laptop and Googled *casein*. And that's when I discovered that the milk sugar in cheese is called the lactose, while the milk protein is called the casein ("*kay-seen*"). Though it is possible to be sensitive to both, usually people can tolerate either the lactose or the casein. Aged cheeses, such as Swiss, no longer hold any milk sugar because it has been eaten and digested by the cheese-making microorganisms during the fermenting process. Aged Swiss is lactose free and is high in protein, in casein.

I was stunned. I raced to the grocery store and straight to the gourmet cheese cooler, standing helplessly over it with no idea where to begin since I hadn't gazed into one of these for fifteen years. A friendly employee helped me locate some aged Swiss, and I took it home to try.

Oh, the wonder of a rich, fragrant cheese after fifteen years! In my mouth it was pungent and smooth, and in my belly it digested with no problem. Bear was right; I could eat lactose-free cheeses.

I got the feeling that some parts of life were being turned inside out; the cheese issue was only one of them. When I commented on this to Bear, he said only, "One doesn't need to look at things the same way. As water can reshape the land, so the waters of spirit can reshape the landscape in an instant."

A few days after the cheese experiment I met for tea with a new acquaintance, a clergywoman in a mainstream Christian denomination. She was seasoned in life and in spirituality, a person who had overcome formidable obstacles, as a woman, to becoming a church leader. I could only imagine that she had led a long and intriguing life of prayer.

The conversation turned toward this new spiritual path I was exploring, and I found myself telling her about Bear's advice on cheese. When I got to the punch line, "And it digested perfectly!" the clergywoman beamed and exclaimed, "How wonderful!" Then she added, "That your subconscious remembered from some long-ago time and put it all together for you right now—isn't that amazing!"

My heart sank. I had expected a woman of the cloth to be comfortable talking about a source outside human knowing—talking, in other words, about God. Was it possible that, for her, God was circumscribed by the human subconscious? I replied slowly that to me it didn't seem to be a matter of the subconscious as we usually understand it. "This is about dialogue. About relationship," I said. She listened politely.

I began to realize how much I had changed when I found myself wanting to ask, Wouldn't a relationship be more fun? Like, aren't two heads better than one? I thought of our own human bodies, our own digestive systems: we thrive because so much of our gut is not "us" but someone else—millions of someone elses, all the microorganisms who do the digesting work for us. Ecologists say that in diversity lies strength; in community, resilience. The world is peopled, I wanted to say, and each kind of person has its own wisdom. To think our subconscious is only a private possession may be as woefully inadequate as considering our own bodies to be only human bodies. What if the thing we call the human subconscious is, like the cells of the human body, 90 percent other-than-human? When creative ideas occur, wouldn't it be more fun to find out *who* they're coming from? Wouldn't it be more comforting to actually see a face?

Later I asked Bear about that conversation in the tearoom. "The twoness is a tricky topic," Bear offered thoughtfully, "because we are not talking about a spirit that is completely separate from the material world. This *is* something more than human knowing," he went on. "At the same time, it is not separate from the body. It is deeply within; it is deeply not within."

The danger, Bear said, lay in collapsing into either pole, thinking that the wisdom we contact through prayer or Journeys is *only* the human subconscious or that it exists *only* outside ourselves. "There are qualities of each," Bear said, "but the point is to keep it in tension. Not same, not separate."

50

From time to time I still shook my head in some disbelief as I took the paw of a bear (for pete's sake!) to go traveling in spirit worlds.

"Why do you show up as a bear?" I asked one day in early October.

"Why not a bear?" he shot right back.

Sometimes I wondered who Bear was, *really*. An amorphous spirit who only looked like a bear to me? Or a "real" bear who had once lived on Earth? Even as I formed the questions, I had to chuckle. Here I was, asking like a medieval theologian, Can God be known in himself or only in how he appears to us? Bear brushed away all such mental gymnastics and hinted that engaging in them would likely take me away from the center of the action. Bear might show up as a male or a female bear, though I experienced him more as a "he" than a "she" and so tended to use the masculine pronoun. Or he might show up as a grizzly bear or a polar bear. The differences, again, served a helpful purpose: whatever was needed in *this* moment to convey the point that Bear wished to communicate *to me* in *this* situation. The Helpers were likely to say other things to other people in other situations. And if I was tempted to see Bear as a little too amorphous, too dematerialized, too "spiritual," he might, with a sly wink or a nod, take me on a Journey to emphasize his bearness.

For instance, one morning in a later year Bear suggested we go visit a river. In the Journey he showed me a massive, roaring mountain river, very bracing and cold. As soon as we waded in—I too became a bear—I could see thousands of salmon jumping upstream around us. We grabbed fish left and right. No sooner had we gobbled one fish than we could grab and feast on another. The experience of gorging was, I discovered, a rare one; a bear apparently spends much of the time feeling either slightly or overwhelmingly hungry. This was the one time in the year when we could stuff ourselves to the limit and then, if we wished, stuff ourselves even more. At last we'd had all that we could eat, and we waded out of the river and wandered into the forest to rest. The Journey ended there.

I opened my eyes and reached for my laptop. Googling "salmon run" just for fun, I discovered that the peak of the salmon run in the Pacific Northwest was taking place that very weekend.

Did I subconsciously know when the salmon return home in the Northwest? Of course it's possible, but more and more I found myself uninterested in this interpretation. I began to see the limitations it placed on the heart—keeping human beings at the center of reality, the anthropocentric focus of all meaning and all meaning-making. Installing ourselves on that throne of knowledge has already brought us to the brink of annihilation. Why would we want to do more of it?

I began to forget just how steely a grip the materialist view had held on me until very recently. I forgot that my devotion to this view had been so strong that I couldn't even see it; I just swam in it like a fish swims in water. And though I'd broken out of it far enough to write a book about communicating with animals, I had remained at the same time so immersed in it that I had accepted the idea of talking with "real" animals but disallowed talking with "spirit" ones. In the years just before I learned to know Bear, the natural-supernatural divide had remained my starting point for understanding the world in spite of the fact that I was writing criticisms of that divide in my own scholarly publications.

The further I went in relating to Bear, the clearer it became that my skeptical outlook had shifted.

"You've been led into a deeper understanding," Bear said one day in early October. "Something fundamental in your paradigm has been dramatically shifted."

The passive voice was intended.

51

Later in the same conversation we began talking about the bears who had died in Boulder. Every autumn, bears who lived in the mountains would wander down into town to raid garbage cans, trying to put on winter fat. After one or two trips into town, a bear would be relocated back up into the mountains, but state law required that a bear who trespassed three times be killed. So far this year in Boulder, four bears had already been slain. I was aghast at the loss of these animals.

Bear was more sanguine. He said in a factual tone, "That is what happens when relationships with the beings in the larger surroundings are not valued. This is a very logical outgrowth of the way human beings—even Boulderites!—have structured their world to ignore the matrix."

I wondered if I'd heard right. *Matrix* was not a word Bear had used before.

"Human beings ignore this larger matrix," he said. "People's vision has been so obscured that they are not able to even see this matrix, let alone imagine how to be good citizens within it."

"So, Bear," I asked, "do you really mean to use that word? Because in the movie"—my long-ago association with the word—"it has a negative quality." It was a false reality conjured up by a cabal of cyberbeings to feed off human energy while keeping humans blind to the illusion. Meanwhile, outside of that false reality, the actual Earth was a charred and desolate place.

Bear called attention to the givenness of the movie matrix—the fact that when humans were "born" to it they entered an already functioning, complex system. He suggested that, in a similar way, there is a quality of givenness, a reality independent of humans, that it would be helpful for us to recognize in relation to—I was going to say "nature," but Bear wanted a more personal word. Each of us is born to the matrix, "is born to it, born to *her*," Bear said, emphasizing the feminine root of the word, *mother*.

He was stretching me here. I didn't like using a feminine pronoun for either Earth or nature. In a culture where the Creator is "he"—and emphatically separate from the creation—calling nature "she" reinforces the old idea that feminine matter is always subordinate to masculine spirit. "Mother Earth" bolsters the notion that women, but not men, nurture the next generation and women, but not men, do the work of care.

But when Bear used the feminine pronoun, he was not referring to physical Earth. He was turning that old inequality on its head. The source itself, he suggested—the reality flowing behind and through the physical world—is like a mother nurturing her children. The source is personal, not mechanical; she brings forth everyone here. To live is to be related by ties of blood and kinship and love. To be here is to belong to a family.

"*She* cares for us," Bear went on. "*She* stimulates our gifts. *She* receives us at the end."

Each of us, he said, must forge our own relationship with this matrix—this living family of forces and personalities and realities surrounding us. Bear said, "When the word *matrix* is used to describe an obviously illusory system, as it was in the movie, then it is a good idea to unmask and get behind the illusion." But he suggested that the illusion under which human beings in the modern world are living is just as powerful and just as illusory as it was in *The Matrix*.

"Get to the *real* matrix," Bear said. "The *real* relationships with your surroundings. Pay attention to how you interact with the bears, how you interact with the weather, how you interact with the earth and fossil fuels."

Except that Bear didn't like the term *fossil fuels* because, as he said, "it turns coal and other layers of geological deposits, which are simply earth-records, into objects to be used in one certain way. It transforms earth-records into a product for human use." The term *fossil fuels*, Bear said, makes it impossible for humans to imagine those fossil layers as having any existence independent of us—and, by implication, makes it impossible for us to leave them in the ground.

Bear preferred a different term. "*Fossil beds*—now that would conjure up more of how they are intended to be viewed, because the word *bed* makes people think of rest and deep inactivity."

Bear encouraged me to go back and look at the whole conversation in these terms: "How language conjures up, creates, a whole pattern-set of meanings and activities and how it embeds those meanings and activities—human projections—into something that may have an entirely other identity." Bear recommended a different approach: "seeing things as they are, beyond those projections. Seeing the *real* matrix, getting beyond the human illusion."

He had one more thing to say: "Language itself is the illusory matrix." It tempts human beings into thinking that we understand things as they are in themselves when in fact, he said, we understand only our own *thinking* about them.

Then he pointed out the window: "You want to go?"

I paused. "After all that, I need a moment to catch my breath."

While I was pausing Bear said, "All this is part of nature." Now he was using the word *nature* deliberately. "All this," he repeated—everything I might see on our travels, the very fact of talking with an unseen Helper—"is part of what humans mean when they talk about nature."

And then we whooshed in spirit to a dense and comfortable darkness—not the twinkling, starlit darkness of the night sky but an encompassing darkness extending to infinity. I felt welcomed and enveloped, as if by a warm and spacious womb.

A sense of self melted away. I perceived vectors of activity—arrows moving outward and sinking back into a sort of fluid, unbounded center, flashing and releasing, some arrows longer, others shorter, each of them a tiny, powerful *whoosh*, all moving randomly to and from this shifting center. The motion was continual and pleasing though completely unpredictable. It occurred to me that this was like the nucleus of an atom with its unending pulses of energy.

I was invited to explore the random motions as long as I wished. As I watched, the sense of motion was joined by a sense of music, so that each arrow flashing through space sounded its own particular note, and all the vectors together made up a marvelously random music that called to mind every corner of the Earth. It had the haunting quality of space music, the vigor of rock, the drumming of African chants, the overtones of marimbas and flutes—every kind of music in a dynamic mix, all random yet somehow fitting together into harmonious and exciting rhythms.

A moment later the various qualities of music shifted into different colors, each shade of color gleaming, as if I had stepped inside a rainbow, and around me every point in space were also a rainbow, and within each of these points were other rainbows, colors within colors, all the way down. I laughed aloud with pleasure.

Finally the colors and motions resolved into an image of points of twinkling light—sharp and fresh as if crystalline. The effect of the whole was aesthetically pleasing—swift motion, unending activity, yet all taking place in a leisurely way, as if moving to its own tempo.

Throughout all these marvels of color and light and sound, one sensation took precedence: unpredictability. Complete, utter unpredictability. Nothing regular at all.

Bear liked that I had picked up on that quality. "A fundamental unpredictability," Bear emphasized. "Whatever line of human thought acknowledges, respects, and preserves that fundamental lack of predictability has something of spirit in it, and whatever lines of thought try to predict and control are misguided," Bear said; "they are not seeing reality clearly."

After we returned from that Journey, almost as an afterthought, Bear offered a postscript: "Einstein was right," he said. "God does not play dice. And yet," Bear added, "Einstein could not quite fathom the inherent unpredictability of the energy, or the God, that he so loved and revered."

I didn't remember that Einstein had loved God at all, so I Googled for a refresher. What Einstein so loved was not a personal God but rather the fundamental structure of nature—how reality is put together. He had pledged his loyalty at an early age to this foundational nature, as it could be understood through science, and it provided his guiding light throughout life. He experienced this core of reality as so dependable and firm that until his death he resisted the quantum mechanics revolution with its claim that nature at the subatomic level can be described only in probabilities.

Bear was saying that in this respect Einstein was right: reality does not run on a gamble. But at the same time, Einstein could not grasp how utterly unpredictable reality actually is, continually running free of human expectations.

Those seventy minutes spent with Bear—first a mind-stretching conversation about language and then a Journey with its glimpse into how nature is put together—left me with a feeling of clarity the rest of the day, as if I could watch each moment arise in turn and clearly see what to do in this one, then this one, then this one. Each thing on my schedule happened with ease. I got the feeling that events in life had the power to guide themselves.

Late in the afternoon I turned to coring apples for dinner and—oops!—promptly stabbed myself in the thumb with the tip of the paring knife. Apparently knives didn't guide themselves after all. Seeing the blood swell and ooze, I made a mental note: watch the use of knives after Journeying.

52

The very next evening after our conversation about bears, I attended a nature film festival at a local auditorium attended by hundreds of nature lovers. Before the screening a speaker invited us all to become quiet. He explained about the four bears slain in recent weeks for wandering into Boulder, and he asked us to observe one minute of silence to honor the bears.

I could almost hear puzzlement circling like a restless buzz around the room: A minute of silence? For *bears?* It was likely the first time most of us there had taken part in such a ritual. I too felt the strangeness.

I closed my eyes, but what I experienced was not silence. Immediately into mind popped an image of Bear jumping up and down, clapping and cheering loudly. I could barely suppress a snicker.

For one minute, hundreds of us kept silence for bears—thanking them for their lives, showing compassion for their deaths, acknowledging that humans had been the cause. Our minute of silence would not bring the bears back or right the skewed relations between bears and humans. But what it did do was remind us—by its very strangeness—that we were used to valuing the lives of humans and bears differently. For one minute, hundreds of us paid our respects to bears.

The next morning I asked Bear why he was so raucous.

"Because it was such an unusual request, it had more impact on people than anything else," Bear said. "Applying a ritual that is usually reserved for humans to other-than-humans was helping to jar people out of a complacency that they didn't even know they had. Any conviction about how things are," he added, "may need to be shaken loose, even and perhaps especially for the converted." A moment of silence for what Bear called the murdered bears? He thought it was brilliant.

"That's an interesting word—*murdered*," I said.

"Well," Bear replied, "it would be a word used in relation to humans." He sent a feeling of gentle teasing: "You should not think yourself exempt from the class of people who have structures to be shaken loose from!"

53

The glimpse Bear had given into the fluctuating aliveness of nature became a lens he used for looking at every experience that October. Whatever took place, Bear related it back to the unpredictability lying at the core of reality, what he called an "unfettered unpredictability."

When I traveled out of town and met with a long-ago friend to tell her about this new path I was on, Bear recommended meeting on new ground rather than in the places where we'd matched up years before. He encouraged me to give her full freedom—even to *not* understand anything I might say. After we met and she responded with openness—she too was extending freedom to me—Bear said, "This is related to those unpredictable motions you saw. That foundational freedom needs to be preserved in each relationship, each situation, each moment, each mind. That willingness to allow," he said, "is key for helping things go right."

Bear added, "There is a big connection here with what the Buddhists talk about in getting past the mind and bringing oneself open, free, to each moment." He suggested that I watch for that core of freedom within people I meet. "Is their core one of listening for those unpredictable waters, or is it one of trying to manage those waters? At a person's core, is there curiosity and openness, or is there certainty instead? Because when someone is certain they know," he added, "it is a small step to manipulating what they know for their own ends. A very small step.

"Spirit is found always in the freedom," Bear went on, "the unpredictability, the ungovernable quality of nature. Which means the natural surroundings into which we are born. Which means every situation, every moment, every being we see, human or tree or animal or anyone. Every molecule, every atom. Ungovernable."

Later in the month, home inspections and other sale-related business took place on our property, though no closing date had yet been finalized. Bear noticed I felt irked about the visits. He was right. They always seemed to fall at the most inconvenient times. I resented not having the power to decide who could walk into my house or when, though I did have to admit we were being handsomely compensated with low rent.

Bear suggested that I was irked instead about our uncertain finances. Some of it might be temporary, he said, "but a certain precariousness characterizes all life on Earth. Those who try to control that precariousness," he added, "are not living in accord with the fundamental unpredictability." Bear suggested I back off from the irked feeling but get fully in touch with the kernel of truth hiding within it: "Rest in the truth of precariousness."

Recently I'd watched a little mouse on the patio scrounging for breakfast. The autumn morning was crisp and clear, with newly fallen leaves lying crinkled at the bases of their trees. Gazing idly from a window, I glimpsed a small movement on the ground and, through binoculars, saw that it was a mouse nosing here and there in the leaf litter. Suddenly she pounced, grabbing a prize and crouching to nibble it. In her paws she clutched the fresh carcass of a yellow jacket. She munched for a few seconds and then, as if she couldn't contain herself, picked up her treasure and scurried a few feet away and nibbled again. Too excited to stay in one place, she picked up the carcass and moved to yet another spot, where she nibbled some more.

Talk about precarious! That humble mouse depends, moment to moment, on whatever gifts become available from the Universe. Bear would return to her in the months to come to underscore just how unpredictable all life on Earth really is. "*Every* being relies on the gifts that become available in each moment," he would say. "Existence is an exercise in entrusting oneself, moment to moment, to the gift of life itself." He suggested that the mouse's delight in receiving her yellow jacket gift is a wonderful example of the delight that human beings could also feel—what he called "delight in casting oneself fully onto the mercy of life. Onto the waves as they unfold. Moment to moment casting oneself onto that great mercy."

That's why riches are such a poison, he added, startling me with his categorical term, because, in his words, "they prevent a person from seeing that mercy and enjoying it." They subtract from the total possible delight in life. They tempt a person to take credit for their own success instead of recognizing that it is, as Bear said, "completely divorced" from their own efforts. Wealth blinds people to the true nature of life, he said. "What an utter blindness that is," he added.

I was reminded of a saying of Jesus: "It is easier for a camel to pass through the eye of a needle than a rich person to enter the kingdom of God."

Feeling financially vulnerable, Bear suggested, was a good thing if it helped Tim and me grow our compassion for others who experience uncertainty. It would also help us remember the true nature of life. "It's all mercy," Bear said. "It's all a gift."

54

One day Bodhi and I, out on our afternoon walk, met up with a woman who was letting her dog run free, flouting the city's leash law. Bodhi is a rescue; he was picked up as a five-month-old stray in a rural area of another state where dogs often run loose, hungry and aggressive. He is terrified of loose dogs. His herding blood also gives him an overdeveloped sense of order, so any dog running free triggers his deep urge to corral them. Though he has grown more confident and calm with age, when it comes to loose dogs he still goes apoplectic. That day Bodhi snarled and barked and lunged with all thirty-five pounds of fear and fury, and it was nearly enough to pull me down.

I called out to the woman, asking her to leash her dog, but she was unconcerned. She waved my request out of her face like a tiresome fly. And that's when I began to feel as snarly as Bodhi. The nerve of her! Putting others in danger for her own convenience! I fantasized all kinds of ways to teach her a lesson.

When I sat down with Bear later I was still growling. Bear was more pragmatic. He suggested that if someone was disobeying a well-known law, it was likely a tiny symptom of a much larger and deeper problem, and the best thing to do was to leave her to her ignorance and move on.

I tried to come into that open, neutral place, ready to listen for a larger wisdom, but it was a struggle. Bear suggested I talk myself through it for the record. He would stand by to help.

"Okay, coming to neutral," I said. "It's like working to step into a clearing and leave the woods behind you. You see a clearing in front of you, you're feeling a bit closed in with all the trees, you'd like to step into the open, but it takes some work, because when you step into the clearing you leave the safety of all those trees and you're wide open. So the thicket of thoughts and mental processes is something that you want to hang on to because it's safe; you can stay hidden there. Stepping into the center takes some bravery. Some willingness to be exposed. Willingness to leave behind the thicket of emotions and assumptions."

I could feel Bear encouraging me on.

"There's also a sense of feeling a lot smaller in the clearing. I have to be *willing* to feel smaller, because when I'm all puffed up with indignation—like now!—I can feel bigger. And leaving behind that righteous indignation leaves you feeling more vulnerable, more exposed. You can see how situations are bigger, more complicated, than you thought."

Bear began to chime in, to call my attention to that ceaseless, unpredictable motion at the heart of things. How coming into that open clearing in meditation is like being willing to accept the fundamental unpredictability at the core of nature. And how that kind of acceptance—the act of giving the Universe its freedom, including giving others complete freedom, even to act poorly if they wish—is a prerequisite for seeing accurately in a Journey. It brings one into closer alignment with the source of aliveness, the source of wisdom, the center of unpredictable arising.

Bear added, "When one has not come into a clearer place than the normal, everyday, busy mind, then the Journey is colored by unhelpful emotions, mistaken assumptions. And so it is up to the individual to clarify their mind, to let things settle out, so that the Journey is as true as possible. And it is up to the individual to be aware of the contours of their own mind so that they can be responsible with their Journeying.

"Stepping out of the thicket and into the clearing," Bear went on, "is not at all a simple process, as you have seen. Many layers of activity and commitment are involved in that one seemingly simple act."

He brought to my mind another saying of Jesus: "Unless you transform and become like a little child, you cannot enter the kingdom of heaven." Those words showed a great deal of wisdom, he said, about how a lifetime of living can predispose people to seeing in ways that are out of touch with reality. To see clearly, a change is needed: toward the mind of a child, toward the beginner's mind that the Zen master Shunryu Suzuki taught. "Just that much openness," Bear said, "just that much trust, just that much depth of curiosity is needed for a Journey that is authentic and that takes one into seeing what is real and new rather than into confirming old patterns of thinking and old prejudices. Living in the new, in the unpredictable: It begins in the clearing. It begins as a little child. It begins with beginner's mind."

Bear had one clarification to make: "Living in the new—in the most enlivening insights—will carry that sense of coming home, like one already knew this at the deepest level of one's being. So," he cautioned, "not to get confused that becoming like a child is about surrendering one's own good sense or judgment. It's about recognizing what has resonance with the deep-springing waters in one's own soul."

I saw again the untamed currents of the flood, the waters seeping anew out of the hill under my feet.

"What is true, what is authentic," he said, "will call forth that deep springing."

55

On the Saturday before Halloween, Tim walked down to the end of the street to visit the buyers of our house and give them a little computer help. During these last months, while I had been talking with Bear, Tim had been training himself in website development, and he was beginning to offer his services to others. The buyers informed him that they planned to go through at last with purchasing our house, and the sale would likely close in December.

That night I went to sleep with one thought: "Well, now would be a really good time for that miracle."

The thought was also a request: "Please?"

56

The following morning an email from the owners of our house was waiting in Tim's inbox, informing us officially of the sale. After some items of house business, the tone shifted.

"Okay, this is a long shot and may sound really stupid to you," they wrote. "You know we still own our house in Santa Fe."

Yes, we'd seen pictures of it—a hundred-year-old adobe at the edge of the city within walking distance of the historic downtown. I had pored over the photographs—those thick earthen walls with doors and windows of blue, a large yard filled with native wildflowers and blue grama grass. They'd lived in that house for twenty years but had not been able to sell it before leaving for Boulder, so it had been rented out since.

"Our current tenants are leaving," they wrote. "Maybe you would like to spend some time in Santa Fe?" If we were interested, they would pay for the move, since we would need to organize their belongings as well as ours.

Tim and I read the note. Each of us at first thought, "Nah. That *is* a stupid idea." But within five minutes we were looking at each other: "Why not?"

We replied that we were interested, and more details followed. Our rent would be exactly the same as in Boulder (still under market value in Santa Fe). The stay in that house would likely be temporary because they intended to sell that property too in another year or so.

On Halloween Tim and I drove the seven hours to Santa Fe and rented an adobe casita near downtown for two nights. That evening I introduced him to Jambo, where we reveled in grilled tilapia and ribs under twinkling orange lights. Our waitress wore a cowboy hat, black miniskirt, and tall black boots with a gun holster strapped to her thigh. Ghosts and vampires patrolled other tables.

By the end of dinner our decision was made. If the house appealed to us, we would turn our lives toward Santa Fe.

The following morning we followed the Santa Fe River to the historic east side and then headed steeply uphill on an impossibly narrow street that in any other town would be called an alley and parked in front of an earthen-plastered wall. We opened the gate and stepped inside.

It looked like an abandoned lot. Four years of drought and trampling by large dogs had not been kind to the grasses and wildflowers of the yard. We walked up the slope toward the front door, past beautiful trees—a tall juniper with room to sit beneath it; some western redbuds; and next to the front door an ancient apricot tree with a graceful, twisted double trunk and gnarled limbs that we'd been told would bloom bright pink in springtime. Yes, the front door was blue. Inside, the house was small, about half the size of our

Boulder house, but it was adobe, with a sweet kitchen and two kiva fireplaces, one in the living room and one in the master bedroom. I was smitten.

We emailed our friends to say we would take the house. We were grateful beyond words. Our search was over.

57

Bear thought the move was a brilliant one, if it appealed to us, and he communicated a happy, gleeful feeling that the house had come to us with such ease. The house—the move itself—was an utter gift. It had appeared out of nowhere. It cast a light a little ways ahead, showing us the next step.

On our second evening in Santa Fe, after deciding we would take the house, I sat in the casita musing along with Bear, listening to the aged wooden vigas in the ceiling creak and groan and thinking about the history of this region. People had been praying on this land, with this land, for thousands of years. Moving here felt like the next step in a pilgrimage. It was a deepening of my path with Bear.

I did feel a little strange that it was a moment of financial uncertainty that had brought the move about. Bear saw it otherwise.

"Who knows," he asked, "what devices the Helpers will use to get someone where they need to go?" If we found the move attractive, we could be grateful for the benefactors who guided us to the right place and not care that being vulnerable had gotten us there. "A time of financial difficulty is a plot device," Bear said; "that's all it is." In the future, he hinted, a good way to regard all kinds of difficulties, either my own or those of others, would be as plot devices. "Cultivating a sense of the mysterious and wondrous plot device keeps one's spirits in the right place," he said, "and allows the process to keep flowing forward."

58

Back in Boulder, in between organizing the next steps in our move, I sat down often with Bear to ponder this miraculous turn of events. Bear preferred instead to reflect on larger themes. He spent about ten days reviewing the ground we had covered this past year.

Recently, I found, I was integrating images from Journeys more easily into daily life. Instead of getting stuck on an interpretation—either feeling flummoxed by the images in a Journey or getting fixed on a purely practical way of understanding them—I was sliding more smoothly between Journeys and everyday life, as if the way between them had been greased a little. I could hold the unknowns of a Journey with more ease. The wisdom gleaned from Journeys was drifting a little more peaceably into daily life.

Bear was jubilant at the progress: "That's it! That's a goal to be sought—to allow the inner pictures, the inner flowering of images, to impinge on the physical world."

He showed me a vapor cloud, once enclosed tight, as if in a balloon, that was now being allowed to expand. As it grew it began to push outward, flowing across the Monopoly board of daily life, elbowing tiny green houses and red hotels out of its way. "It's necessary to allow the vapor to push things away," Bear said, "because one begins to grasp the enormity of it—the largeness, the spaciousness of it—by letting it push against the boundaries of everyday life, over here and over there and there and there. All the way around this cloud it will push against those boundaries." The goal was to give the cloud room to grow, or as he put it, "to allow the richness of the Journeys to expand until they take over the landscape of everyday life."

The words *take over* were an overstatement, he quickly explained. They were intended to convey the sense of opening to something large and rich instead of trying to reduce a Journey to a few useful points, which Bear said was a widespread tendency.

"That is why," Bear said, "we work on the relationship first." Once the relationship with their Helper is well developed, a person is less tempted to try to manage the richness of the images or to reduce the value of a Journey by applying it in a merely utilitarian way—in the way the ego wants to make sense of it. Journeys have a lot more to offer than just their immediate message. "If finding the utility in a Journey is the guiding value," Bear added, "it is easier for the ego to remain in charge; it's easier for the mind to retain control.

"One opens before this magical unfolding," he emphasized. "One does not bend it to one's will." He drew my attention, again, to the utter unpredictability glimpsed in that October Journey. "If the fundamental state of reality is to be like *that*," Bear said, "then to be in accord with reality, one cannot be trying to manage and direct and control. One can only partner. One can observe, one can receive, one can collaborate. But trying to bend that reality is going against the fundamental quality of reality itself."

The goal, instead, is to open to the dance.

59

Opening to the dance was what I had tried to do for years with dream images. Most of my life—until taking up this path with Bear—had been spent living close to dreams, puzzling over them, dwelling as long as possible between sleeping and waking to glean as much from the night as I could. Bear from the start had been nudging me away from that practice. During my very first phone meeting with Chris two years earlier, when I lay down on the bed to feel more relaxed, the Helper had whispered into her ear that I needed to sit up instead, to be more awake. (This advice was addressed to me in particular; what works best for others may be different.)

Now and then over this past year Bear had suggested that it was good to keep in mind the differences between the dream realms and what he was showing me in Journeys. He had spoken about how, in sleep, one's awareness drifts further away from waking life, further toward what he called "the many-layered activities of the Universe." For those activities, there simply do not exist adequate pictures. "That's why dreams seem garbled," he had said; "they are distant approximations of those more distant realities."

Now he added that dreams could lead me down some unhelpful detours. "One can chase a dream image that may not be all that useful," Bear said, "because either it comes out of an unfinished portion of the psyche or it's working off steam or it's about something that is too far removed from daily life," belonging to those more distant mysteries of the Universe. "Dreams are a mixed bag," he added, "some useful, some not so much."

By contrast, on this path the Journey images came from a Helper and were fully designed to provide the best nourishment possible. Because they originated with a Helper rather than, for instance, a wandering piece of the human psyche, they could be trusted, every one of them, to be helpful. An image would provide insight even when it required some conscious work to understand and absorb its nuances. It might be packed with many interrelated meanings, Bear said, and the complexity was intended to provide a fun challenge, a gift for the mind to unwrap slowly, layer by layer.

"That's why the emphasis in *this* path," he said, "is on being awake, physically awake: tackling this with the conscious mind."

"That's an interesting word, Bear," I said. "*Tackling* this."

"Some grappling is normal and to be expected," he replied, "and one needs full conscious awareness to come to terms with the path and to stay grounded, in touch with reality."

60

One day Bear invited me to get some close-up views of him. I looked carefully: his large snout, lighter and more honey colored than the rest of his face; his enormous teeth; the small rounded ears; the shaggy fur, shaggier than I expected; those—oh, my—gigantic claws, a set of steak knives in each paw. "Helpful in eating and defending," Bear smiled. All was offered in a spirit of great affection.

"What is it about being able to see a bear body?" I asked.

"How helpful it is to have an other," Bear responded. "The benefit of imagining spirituality as developing a relationship with an other."

Then Bear suddenly took off ahead of me, ambling across a landscape of golden-yellow grasses, inviting me to follow. He wanted to clear up some misconceptions about what *following* means. "For modern people the idea of following conjures up notions of following in a slavish fashion," he said, "doing what a person has been told to do, because this society decided it wants to structure most relationships in a top-down way."

I thought of everything from office managers to college administrators to the big boss in the sky.

"It's more like following somebody who knows the territory,"

Bear said while I watched his substantial rear end lumbering through the grass ahead of me. "It's more like going outside to play with your best friend. She saw something that she wants to show you, and she has an idea of how much fun it will be." And Bear stopped walking and sat down, pulling up clumps of grass and munching. Then he lay down and rolled in the grass. He sat up again and explored nearby plants, chewing on the tasty ones. I became a bear too, rolling in the dirt and chewing idly, finding a rocky outcrop on which to scratch my back. It was a lazy golden day, and we were just having fun.

Then the scene shifted, and a few minutes later it shifted again, and finally it came to rest in soft darkness. "*Following*," Bear said, "means following the interior images as they shift. Being willing to travel where the arising and fading images want to lead. Paying attention to the shifting images of a Journey," he added, "is good practice in staying attentive to the fresh springing of the world.

"This *is* the creativity of the world," Bear went on. "This is the creativity of matter, that every piece of it—all the way down as small as you can go and all the way as large as you can go—partakes of the fresh springing. Following images in the mind gives a person a more palpable sense of those unpredictable motions at the center of reality, which otherwise seem nebulous.

"The interior images," he added, "are the story form of the fresh springing."

61

Bear said that having a recognizable "someone" at the other end of this communication line was useful for human beings not only because we are such social creatures but also because humans today have such a hard time remembering the aliveness of the world. "It comes back to relationship," he said. "A person at the other end of the line is a continual reminder that 'things' are alive—springing, imparting their own wisdom—in ways that human beings these days have forgotten." He went on, "It's not just useful, but it's closer to how things actually are; it's closer to reality. Everybody *is* awake."

He suggested that many kinds of people would benefit from contacting the Helper at the end of their own line. "If you are a web geek," he said; "if you are a mother or father; if you are a lecturer; if you are a bricklayer; if you are a fitness consultant; if you're a hiker. Everybody has the experience of being aware of a little voice inside that is wiser and kinder and stronger and softer and happier and calmer than their usual frame of mind. So *this* path," Bear said, "is about making conscious contact with that voice. Finding out who is on the other end of the line. And developing that relationship on a daily basis so that the kinder, calmer, stronger wisdom is available continually.

"But it takes quieting," Bear added, "and it takes accommodating oneself to a new relationship."

62

The caveat to all this talk of relationship, of course, was that the Helpers are not completely separate from the self. Months ago Bear had called himself "the source of the I," a phrase that had continued to intrigue me. I'd been mulling it off and on ever since. How was Bear the source of the self? How were Bear and I related? How is any person related to their Helper?

Bear said that for some people and some societies, it's most helpful to emphasize how close spirit is to the self. By contrast, for those who grasp the closeness and connection, it's more helpful to emphasize twoness. In my case, since I had spent a lifetime trying to heal that split in my society's thinking between God and nature, between spirit and self—in other words, now that I had a good grasp on the not-two aspect—it was worthwhile to explore the not-one character of spirit. The relationship aspect. The presence of an other.

This morning Bear's presence wrapped me even more than usual in warm affection. He sent a feeling of deep connection and camaraderie. It was a preface to talking about healing that divide— bringing the unseen realms closer to the physical world so that the warm connection might take root in more people's lives.

"When Western society renounced the worlds of spirits," Bear said, "even demonizing them, a great retreat took place from unseen realities. It has had a profoundly chilling effect on the human spirit." He emphasized the word *chilling* to contrast with the affection he was sending my way. There was a direct connection, he said, between the retreat from spirit and the tendency of people to become less loving and supportive of one another and colder as well toward the natural world.

It was a new thought. I'd reflected many times on how societies in which people become cold toward each other, allowing some to suffer while others profit, also forget their natural surroundings, while the opposite is just as true: societies that ignore or break their connections with nature also break their connections to one another. But Bear was saying something different: forgetting spirit makes people coldhearted.

"I've never thought of it that way," I said.

"Well, you've been edging toward it for some time," he replied. "'Finding tongues in trees,'" he said, quoting one of my favorite lines from *As You Like It*, "is part of the journey toward reacknowledging the land of spirit."

"'Land of spirit'—that phrase gave me goose bumps!" I said.

"That's because *land* and *spirit* are so divorced from each other in the thinking of this society," Bear replied. "Land implies spirit," he went on. "Look at a tree, and there is no need to look 'beyond,' as people think. The spirit is not beyond, the spirit is right there. Spirit is implicated in every piece of visible nature, every living thing, every naturally occurring piece of the world." Even rocks, he said, unlike the artifacts of human making, have their own purposes and vectors, their own intrinsic upwelling life.

"The growing edge for people in this society, even those who are attuned to the divine, is to make space for the unseen—to make it visible, audible, explicit, in everyday life."

He had a few suggestions: "Acknowledge the presence of spirit, not just when you walk on a trail or sit outside, but even indoors, in the middle of human gatherings. Acknowledge the presence of the animals, the trees, the wider world of spirit."

Then Bear gestured over his shoulder to the window behind him: "Want to come?" He paused for a moment so that I could focus again on the question I'd been mulling that morning: How were Bear and I related?

"Sure, let's go," I said.

We zoomed out, out, out, away from Earth, outside the atmosphere, to a point in deep space where we could look back on the planet as a whole. Around us was the deep night, black and velvet, twinkling with millions of faraway suns busy lighting other worlds. Bear called my attention to how I would feel if I were an astronaut who had traveled physically to this point in space, floating free of the Earth. I would be separated from everything familiar, all I hold dear. I would suddenly realize, in a way that is much harder to realize when the feet are planted firmly on the ground, that the Earth is the source of all—the source of my own life, the source of every other life-form I interact with, the source of every meaningful relationship I have ever experienced. I would feel a tremendous pull toward the Earth as the source.

In the Journey I experienced that great pull as love. It was gravity, but it was love as well. Bear seemed to emphasize the similarity between them—maybe more than a similarity. The pull of gravity toward the center of the Earth was like the spirit-pull toward the source of love and meaning. Love and gravity, the pull to the source.

Other things too were part of this pull. Going on Journeys with Bear was a pull to the source. Delighting in life, in the natural world, was a pull to the source.

"The pull of the source is love," Bear said. "Do you wonder how we are related?" he added. "It's the pull to the source."

And then he stopped—before I could quite wrap my understanding around his words.

"Just play with it," he said. He encouraged me to think of it often: "Love as the pull to the source." To take it with me as a lens for focusing the moments of the day. "Because, after all," he added, "we're just talking about pictures. This is not the thing itself; this is just pictures. So play with pictures, and see what effects they have."

63

If listening to a Helper was as simple as listening to the voice of an unseen friend, Bear wanted to emphasize one caution. "Listening to another human being," he said one day, "is far inferior to listening to the Helpers."

I asked, "Are you talking about taking on gurus and teachers?"

"Taking on a teacher," Bear replied, "can be very different from listening to a teacher as the voice of God." One didn't need to confuse a teacher with the source; it was entirely possible to take on a guru while retaining an independence of mind and heart. He only meant to say that in any tradition where the focus is on a human teacher, such a confusion becomes tempting.

Bear called it "being blinded by station," the act of trusting the words and views of certain individuals not because they are inherently wiser than other people but because of their social position. Perhaps they occupy a role of authority or prestige, or they are a member of one's own family, or one esteems them for some other reason. It is important, he said, "not to confuse esteem with the voice of the divine." He added, "Obviously some people are wiser than others, and some people deserve to be listened to. The difference is whether one is listening and using one's own judgment, or listening and taking on someone else's view of things as the Truth," with a capital *T*. "It is a misstep," he added, "to redirect one's own connection with spirit through another person, thereby losing one's independence."

But he had a few things to add about how this temptation to be blinded by station can show up in subtler ways as well. For instance, there was the tongue-tied feeling I often got on the phone with Chris when she asked me to enter into a Journey with Bear. At home in the privacy of my closed room, the Journeys would flow easily, but on the phone, when I heard Chris say, "Would you like to ask Bear directly about that?" my tongue would cower on the roof of my mouth and my brain go blank. I would feel cornered, on the spot. Bear said it was related to the stage fright I'd experienced as a musician decades earlier.

"This is a piece of performance anxiety," Bear said. "It's a little worry about how one is seen."

By now I knew what to do with these more pointed messages from Bear. "So, Bear, do you have anything more to show me about this tendency to worry about how I will be seen?"

Bear showered me with a feeling of great amusement, a big chuckle that also conveyed deep support. "Be ready to laugh at yourself for this one," he said. "That will keep things in balance better than anything else.

"Remember," he added, "that the Helper's guidance is always supportive and loving. Keep that feeling of Bear's arm around your shoulders. Remain in that feeling of support."

64

Around the middle of November, a month before we were to leave
Boulder, the work of moving swung into full gear—sorting, purging,
selling, packing. And that's when Bear began showing up for our
conversations dressed for vacation—ambling down a beach in board
shorts and cool sunglasses with a surfboard under his arm. I laughed
out loud, which seemed to be the point.

Bear asked if I wanted to learn to surf. I said, "Definitely!" and
suddenly found myself in the waves lying on a board, paddling out
toward deeper waters.

Bear suggested I practice getting up on the board first, finding
my balance. "Just let the waves do their thing without getting too
involved with them," he suggested.

After a few minutes I got the feel of it—how to rise to standing
with little fuss or to-do and then balance on the board as it rode the
surface of the water.

Bear said we would leave the bigger waves for another time.
"Notice the state of mind when one is riding the surface," he said.
"It's relaxed and easygoing, not trying too hard."

I could feel the ease in my body, the sense of being carried above the water. This apparently was an excellent frame of mind to hold throughout the moving process.

"Let the waves of change just happen," he said. "Ride the surface."

Then Bear called my attention to his cool shades. He was still wearing them. The surfing we'd been doing was so easy that he'd never been in any danger of losing them. When it came time to climb off our boards, it happened effortlessly. We rode the boards to shallow water and stepped off them into the sand for an easy walk to shore.

"Keep that feeling of ease in the body," Bear advised, "not grappling too hard with anything"—not the thick editing job I'd agreed at last to take on, not the farewell Thanksgiving potluck we would host at our house in a few days for a table of twelve, not the move, nothing at all. He threw out a tantalizing question: "Just how easy could this move be?"

The next day Bear again showed up in board shorts on the beach. This time we walked up and down the water's edge, soothed by the spacious sky, lulled by the rhythms of the waves. Then Bear lay down in the sand, and so did I, wriggling into the warmth beneath our backs.

I practiced keeping that feeling of ease.

65

I can't say the move was easy, though it did take place with no major mishaps, for which I was grateful. Wacky moments threatened now and then to run it off-kilter, one of them while I was driving to our new home with Bodhi.

It was the second Saturday in December. The movers had packed their truck and departed on Thursday, and Tim had flown to New Mexico on Friday to meet and unload the truck today. I'd spent my last day in Boulder making endless trips to recycling centers and thrift stores and then stuffing unredeemables into the garbage can of the neighbor who had conspired with me in dandelion parties and now dragged his large container down the street to help. It was the most thoughtful thing I could imagine anyone doing. I made a mental note: remember how much help people need clearing out odds and ends after their moving van leaves.

I camped out on the floor of the empty house and after a few hours of sleep awoke at four on Saturday morning to pack the car. Coolers full of fridge contents, bedding in black plastic garbage bags, the Wi-Fi equipment and last-minute boxes that didn't make it onto the truck filled our Subaru to overflowing, with only half a seat of free space remaining in the back for Bodhi. Just before leaving the house I placed my oriole feeder on the counter and wrote a note: "The orioles come with the house." Then it was time to pick Bodhi up from the sitters, where he'd stayed for three nights at his favorite ranch in the mountains.

By nine thirty Bodhi and I were off. I was due at eleven at the nature center of a state park south of Denver to participate in a book reading and reception for local nature writers. I would be on time but just barely.

Why had I accepted an invitation like this? Well, it was right on the way, and moving itself was crazy, so why not?

At five minutes to eleven, we pulled up to the gate of the state park, and I told them who I was.

The attendant's eyes shifted to the backseat. "I'm sorry, I can't let you in. We don't allow dogs."

I again explained who I was, that they were expecting me inside for a reading, and that Bodhi was with me because we were right now moving to Santa Fe. The gatekeeper phoned ahead to the office. I sat and watched the minutes tick by. At last the attendant returned.

"No, I'm sorry."

I asked to speak to the staff on the phone. I explained my story again, and then once more.

Finally the park director understood. "Oh, you're moving now! Today!"

"That's right," I said, and mentally thanked Bear for helping me grow patience this year.

The director explained that they were strict about dogs because any pets in cars would draw mountain lions to the parking lot, and he kindly promised the staff would keep an eye on Bodhi in the car while I was occupied.

The book event was as fun as I'd hoped it would be, and then Bodhi and I continued on to New Mexico.

Bodhi is a pacing, panting traveler. With no room to maneuver in the packed backseat, he stood in one place, panting in my ear and dripping saliva onto my shoulder, most of the remaining hours to Santa Fe. I cracked the windows wide to give him fresh air and drove wearing woolly hat and gloves to keep from freezing in the wintry blasts. I was as grateful as he was for potty breaks, where we both could walk on firm ground, even in icy winds, and feel again our connection to the Earth.

Long after nightfall we finally pulled into Santa Fe. A few inches of snow had fallen some days earlier, and remnants of white lingered here and there. Ah, the luminarias!—outlining adobe rooftops, lighting the night with their soft orange glow. Piñon smoke wafted throughout town. I took deep drafts of it, relishing what had just become the smell of home.

In front of our new house, Bodhi jumped out of the car and sniffed footprints in the snow. His tail began wagging furiously, and when I opened the gate he ran straight to the front door. Inside, Tim had been busy. The living area was already set up with rugs and furniture, and Bodhi's favorite blankets and toys were waiting for him. Bodhi moved in as if he had never left home.

On Christmas Eve Tim and I bundled up in down coats and walked to Canyon Road, where the many art galleries along the street hosted an annual Canyon Walk. Luminarias created in the

traditional way—brown paper bags with votive candles set in sand—
glowed in long rows up and down the street, outlining every walk-
way and building. Enormous cottonwood trees, bare of leaves,
twinkled with more lights. Here and there people had lit small bon-
fires in the street, a traditional act of devotion to help guide Mary
and Joseph toward shelter at the end of their long journey. Thirty
thousand people milled along the dark street, their steps guided by
the flickering light of thousands of candles. People paused at galleries to warm themselves and gathered in small groups around bon-
fires to sing Christmas carols. We joined the pilgrimage up and
down the street, bumping elbows, singing carols, stopping in at galleries, grateful to live in this magical place.

Later that week, when I unpacked my pottery from its many
boxes and placed it on the adobe shelves plastered with pink-tan
earth, the pots looked as if they had been created just for this house.

During morning or afternoon walks with Bodhi, I gazed up at
the foothills of the Sangre de Cristos, the southernmost tip of the
Rockies, lying just east of town. In the months to come I would
explore their shadowy forests, enjoy their sunburned trails with
expansive views, be amazed that the winds and weather, because of
those mountains, arrived in town from every which direction.

One late afternoon, walking Bodhi on a nearby street, I gazed
again at the mountains. They were glowing bluish lavender in the
setting New Mexico sun. I was already getting used to watching the
sun rise behind these mountains from our patio door. Suddenly,
scanning the soft ridge, I noticed something I hadn't seen before:
tucked into one hollow was a line of four tiny hills.

Vision and reality slid together and clicked as one. These were the mountains Bear had shown me months earlier, the mountains behind which the sun rose. This was the peaceful place where Bear had advised, "Stay close to that sense of possibility." Chills crept up and down my spine.

"Thank you," I whispered.

66

One morning near the end of December, I woke early and found myself musing about the distance between spirit and matter that Bear and I had talked about so many times this past year. How could that gap be bridged? How could the grip of the mechanistic way of thinking be loosened?

In Journey that morning Bear offered some clues. He said that the mechanistic view is easy to spot because there is an absence of love; there is only use. "Love, respect, connecting—these are what you do with an ensouled world," he said. "This is how you act in a living world, a world always springing with its own intrinsic life. But remove love from the picture, and you're left with only use. A machine can be used until it wears out."

Bear invited me to think back through history, to look for the absence of love in social exchanges to find out just how old the use-based worldview actually is. We thought together back to the Roman Empire, an era I'd studied years before in graduate school. Roman society, rather like today's, offered people a whole smorgasbord of spiritual options in the form of teachers and groups following every conceivable kind of devotion. But no matter what philosophy people held, what god or goddess they followed—or none at all—everyone took part in the same everyday rituals: people in Roman society practiced magic. Spells and charms, potions and amulets and incantations filled their lives. One day in a lovesick haze they might buy a potion to bind a lover, the next an amulet to ward off dangers on the road, the day after that a spell to unlock the mysteries of the future. Every possible misfortune had its charm, every kind of love its own spell. Philosophers and religious leaders alike may have frowned on magic, but their disdain did little to stop people from engaging in it every day.

In modern society we talk of all this magic as "supernatural." It is the error that people inevitably fall into, we think, if they crack the door—even a little bit—to an other-than-physical reality. But that morning Bear suggested something much more interesting: that the Roman magic was mechanistic instead. Every piece of magic, he suggested, was aimed at control—bending nature to human will, controlling another person, forcing the hand of time. "The writing of recipes and spells and magical potions," he said, "had everything to do with using other creatures and very little to do with love for them."

He added that one could think of slavery, also prevalent in the Roman Empire, in the same way. "An empire is built on the backs of others," Bear said, "and therefore it is *nothing* about love."

I heard the absolute statement, unusual for Bear. "*Nothing* about love, Bear?"

"To siphon off the goodnesses of the creatures so that some have so much and others have so little has *nothing* to do with love." He said it with emphasis. Then he added, "This is not in accord with nature's bounty." He repeated, "Where there is regard for the other's welfare, that is love. Where there is not regard for the other's welfare, that is deadness—evidence of belief in an uninspirited, uninspired world." The implication was clear: the presence of slavery, like the presence of magic, is a tipoff to a mechanistic view.

"A living world," he said by way of contrast, "is evidenced by a regard for the interweaving of all creatures." When people lose sight of love, he said, it makes room for many kinds of distortions. "One of those distortions," he added, "goes in the direction of what people recognize as superstition—losing touch with what is real.

"Uses of nature become superstitious when love is absent," he said, "when they tend toward that mechanistic use of others."

Then he introduced a new thought, making a sudden connection with today: "Potions and spells were a use of other creatures without regard for their welfare. Factory farms today are a use of other creatures without regard for their welfare."

I paused to let that sink in. Factory farms, like superstition, grow from a mechanistic view. Putting the two side by side suggested an equivalence I had never considered. Factory farms, rooted in modern materialism, are as far removed from what is real as were the superstitions of premodern times.

He summed up: "Love and use. Two opposite ways. Keeping love in the equation is key."

67

On New Year's morning I woke up at four thirty with a pounding heart, terrified.

Of what? I thought about the day, the week ahead. There was that editing job waiting on my desk, partially done. I wasn't enjoying the work quite as much I used to.

That's when it hit me. This oldest of my work identities was about to slip away. Editing had sustained me through grad school, had served as the one constant throughout my adult life while living situations shifted and partners came and went. Editing was the work that had prepared me for writing, had given me ten thousand hours of writing practice even before I sat down to write a book. I might keep doing it and even enjoying it in the future, but editing would not be the hook on which I would hang my professional hat. Without any clear picture of what that hook or that new hat *would* look like, I felt at loose ends. Too wide open. Unplugged enough to start my heart racing.

I crept out of bed into the bathroom, to avoid waking Tim, and crouched on the bathroom rug to keep warm, thumb-typing into my phone.

Was it possible that I clung this tightly to having a professional identity? Was it possible that even this clinging would have to go?

In a recent session with Chris, Bear had shown her a picture of himself holding above his head an object of great value, a treasure. In the same moment that he was bearing aloft this treasure, a part of him was roaring, "I do not like it!" Another part of him was whimpering, "What is wrong with me that no one else is like me?" Yet through it all Bear just kept a steady hold on his treasure, carrying it forward.

I recognized the picture. It was me. Except, unlike Bear, I hadn't kept a very steady hold on my treasure. I might grasp it stubbornly in one phase of life then completely forget it in another. This morning, shaken awake by terror, I felt closer to whimpering: "How can I hold it aloft when I don't even know what it looks like?"

The question, of course, though I wouldn't see it clearly for months, was really about me: What do I look like? That morning, terror provided some glimmers. The treasure that required me to give up everything in its pursuit was beginning to feel uncomfortably close to home, as if it might be the very self I'd lived with from birth and could never escape. How fitting—that the mysterious angel we wrestle with through the night, who will not let us go and will not reveal its name, turns out to be the very person we thought we knew best.

I couldn't yet see the months ahead—months of walking with Bodhi up and down narrow Santa Fe streets, under trees that rained pink blossoms, past carved wooden doors and earthen walls draped in lilac and wisteria. I couldn't see the flowering of Journeys that lay

ahead and how my relationship with Bear would deepen—a tremendous gain that would often arrive disguised as loss, since there
were many layers of relinquishing left to do, and each letting go
would sting. I couldn't yet see the discomfort I would live in for two
more long years, saying good-bye to roles that were familiar without
being given anything to replace them—anything, that is, except
the joy of bending close to the earth while gardening, watching yellow coneflowers and red Mexican hats bloom in the yard, coaxing
blue grama grass back into thickness, and lying down in a late-
summer dawn among its clouds of golden curling eyelashes. The joy
of wide-open New Mexico skies with thunderclouds that marched
across the desert and unloaded gushing rains. The joy of cottonwoods and aspens so bright with gold in autumn that the eye could
barely stand to look. The joy of winter snow sprinkled delicate as
lace across the ground. And of course the joy of orioles chattering
and squawking as they arrived in spring at my new feeder to gulp
grape jelly, along with western tanagers iridescent in orange and
yellow, and other birds I'd never seen before—evening grosbeaks
with bright-green bills and Virginia's warblers and Bewick's wrens
and even a white-eyed vireo with its burbling, two-phrase melody.
The joy, at last, of simply breathing. In and out. Of welcoming a
new moment, a new day.

Crouched on the bathroom rug on New Year's Day, I asked,
"What is left when the identities are gone? What is the purpose?"

Bear's clear thought arose: "Just enjoy life." And another
thought: "If you can become comfortable in this no-place, this will
be the biggest step of all toward the real." A sense of consolation

flowed into me, and I heard Bear say, "This is what we have been working toward, the loss of identity. This is the beginning of the real path. The spirit path."

I remembered Baba and his advice: "Find the sweetness in the bitterness." Funny, I thought, this doesn't feel all that bitter. Frightening, yes—too wide open. But not bitter. I thought too of Teresa of Ávila, for whom the soul was like a castle carved of diamond, holding many rooms, with the Beloved waiting in the innermost sanctuary.

Yes, this path had been walked by others—others who knew how to find the center, that elusive, insistent center.

The feeling of consolation was followed almost immediately by a new thought from Bear: "Now the fun can begin! When a person realizes that the path is just one of daily communion with what-is, that is the point. Let the fun begin!"

A feeling of allowing arose in me. Of letting myself be propelled in a direction I wouldn't have chosen on a current I couldn't predict. Most of all, of allowing myself to be carried as I go.

In that place where waters spring, always fresh, always free, I said yes.

Afterword

Before I embarked on this path with Bear, I suspected that there is more to this world than meets the eye. Now I find that what we don't know and can't see is simply staggering.

Many times since that first year, Bear has returned to one theme: how intimately joined are the worlds of spirit and nature (physical nature), so closely joined as to be the same thing.

"This world is infused with spirit," Bear said just last week. "Spirit is the juice that gives it life. This world never exists outside of spirit."

I saw an image of a planet enveloped in an atmosphere that was at the same time the infusing fuel of the planet itself.

"Nothing takes place outside of that loving, infusing presence," Bear said. "That *is* what gives the world its being, its flow, its life. It's what makes it run."

Bear went on to say that there are two ways of getting in touch with that flow, and both of them involve reconnecting with nature. (1) One can get in touch with the senses—going outdoors and filling one's senses with the richness of the physical world. Rubbing elbows with so many different beings and so many different ways of being alive, he said, stimulates the core of a person, helping it wake up, helping that person reclaim more of their own unique way of being alive. (2) Or one can listen for the wisdom of spirit, the voice of the Helper, who helps one connect to the larger loving presence that holds and powers and flows through the visible world. This too is connecting with nature.

Bear recommended both avenues. "Though to human beings they seem like two different moments or two different activities," he said, "in fact they are not. They are the same. Not only *are* they the same, they take you to the same place. Two ways of getting in touch with that flow.

"The mistake comes," he added, "when people forget the intimate connection between those two things, believing either that the physical world is all there is or the spirit world is all there is. And either direction leads people away from the greatest love, the greatest mystery, which is that it's all the same thing. It's all bound up together. Inseparable."

So entwined are matter and spirit that when people reconnect with the physical world—with their senses—it brings them closer to spirit. "If people are out of touch with their senses," Bear said recently, "it means they are out of touch with spirit, namely, their own wellsprings. The process of coming back to health is one of lacing senses and spirit together again so the person is not floating outside their body, outside their own purpose."

Coming back to the senses is so crucial, Bear said, because it returns people to themselves and especially to their own perception. "This is the way in which perception is the most trustworthy thing on the planet," he added, "because it is a coming into one's own

body, one's own way of knowing, one's own heart, one's own enjoyment, one's own love. It settles a person in that center."

Simply getting in touch with the senses would provide healing for
many of modern people's ills, he continued. "The healing that fearful
people need can begin by coming back to their senses. The healing
that busy people need is coming back to their senses. The healing that
intellectual people need is coming back to their senses. The healing
that people who pursue money need is coming back to their senses.

"This is why nature is the big panacea," he added.

"Panacea?" I said. "No—um, Bear, that has the overtone of
something not quite real."

Bear shot me a glance then grunted, "Look it up."

Oh, he meant etymology. *Pan* would mean "all," but what about
the rest of the word?

"The everything-remedy," Bear said. "The cure-all."

As soon as the Journey ended, I headed to the dictionary.
Panacea, from the Greek *pan*, "all," and *akos*, "remedy." *Panacea*, the
cure-all.

That Bear.

"Nature is a cure-all," he repeated. "That's why nature is helpful
for grieving people," he added, calling to mind the weekly hikes I'd
participated in long ago after a family member died. "It brings them
back to their own senses, which is a painful place for a grieving person to be. Walking in nature gives them a way of dwelling in the
physical world that is pleasurable, and therefore it shows them the
way out of their misery. A little path opens up, a way to be in the
body that is more peaceful than the grief."

If a person is too busy—and according to Bear just about everyone in modern society is too busy—walking or sitting in nature can restore them to the speed of the body, the organic tempo of life. People who are fearful can benefit from experiencing the steadiness of the ground, the dependability of daily rhythms.

"So nature," he said, "by bringing people back to their senses, actually brings them back to spirit, back to trust in the bigger picture, in the unseen parts of life."

Societies, just like individuals, can fall ill, according to Bear. If people are living in mean-spirited times, he suggested the cause is widespread fearfulness. He gestured around his head in a chaotic way, as if being pestered by angry bees. "If people follow nasty leaders," he said, "it's because of listening to the nasty buzz inside their own heads. People have to turn and listen to different influences. Their own hearts have to dwell in a different place. If a significant portion of the society is listening to the angry buzz, then it behooves that society to consider itself ill and to take steps to heal its illness and bring itself into a happier place."

Bear listed a few symptoms of social illness: "Inequality makes people unhappy. Pursuing money makes people unhappy. Being frightened of others who are different makes people unhappy." Each of them, he said, makes it impossible for people to feel their own agency. In a situation of inequality, people feel unable to affect the world around them. People who are pursuing the ephemera of money feel unable to get enough. Frightened people feel unable to protect themselves. "The only remedies are: Come back to the body; come back to nature; come back to the self; come back to the things that matter, the intangible things that matter." Come back, in other words, to the senses, to spirit.

Many people call this path "shamanism," and I sometimes call it that myself. But what this path is, really, is a path of listening. Listening to the heart. Listening for more-than-human wisdom. Making room for that still small voice. Listening, for me, turns out to be the puzzle piece that slips into place with the ease of water flowing downhill.

"That fit is the thing to keep going toward," Bear said recently about any of the big things we search for in life—a partner or a place to live or a role to fill. "Move toward the fit, and don't stop until you can recognize it and welcome it."

But, I asked, what if it looks like it is out of reach?

"If it's a fit," he replied, "it will be made possible. You go for the fit," he repeated, "and the rest becomes possible."

Ability to hear the quiet voice of the Helper grows—as in any relationship—by setting aside time to respectfully get to know the other. Because this relationship is less tangible than human friendships, it is even more delicate. Concerns of daily life can easily muffle the Helper's unobtrusive voice. Hearing that voice clearly means continually making room—room for the body to breathe, room for the mind to grow quiet, room to feel again the subtler nudges of the heart.

Just a few days ago Bear led me in a Journey through one of his roundabout pathways. He suggested I first bring to mind any half-formed questions or impressions from daily life. My mind ran through a few of them—Bodhi's knee injury, now healing; how to write the next blog post. Bear didn't pick up on these threads, though, and I began to wonder—as so often before—if my mind was wandering.

Finally Bear came clear: this was an exercise in just listening. Life had recently become busier, with more of my attention devoted to that pointed, focused awareness. I needed time to settle again into the Helper's presence and notice the subtler impressions. "Allowing the less-prominent impressions to percolate to the surface in the presence of the Helper," Bear said, "does something important in the psyche." He showed me a picture of a rough-hewn dinghy floating on a river. Giving those subtler impressions room to grow helps to seat a person's dinghy more firmly in the water—as if glued to the currents, able to ride them with more ease. A person can hear their Helper's voice more clearly. "So often the world of the Helpers is seen as an alternate reality," Bear added, "when in fact it's often just a more-forgotten layer of experience."

This path of listening fits within "shamanism" as religion scholars use the word, though I don't know how it compares, if at all, with the listening to nature done by people in other places or times or the shamanisms they may have practiced. I think of my Germanic grandmothers and grandfathers in central Europe more than two thousand years ago, before being Mennonite, before even being Christian: Did they listen in this way? Perhaps some of them did. Germanic tribes regarded certain hills and trees (and posts and pillars) as sacred, though they were also quick to see monsters in the seas and in other overwhelming places. They also worshipped a harsh god of war and performed occasional human sacrifice. I do not feel much kinship with their rites and beliefs, what little is known of them.

Yet a modern form of listening to animal Helpers may hold a certain kinship with even more ancient ways—the animal-venerating traditions of hunter-gatherers. After all, Europeans, like other peoples of the Northern Hemisphere, named the stars at the zenith of the sky after bears, and it is not hard to imagine them claiming the Great Bear and Little Bear as the protectors ambling in their leisurely circuit overhead, forever watching over those who walk the Earth. Old European stories surviving to this day say that humans descended from bears, and in certain European villages, people dressed as bears and other animal helpers still bestow annual good-luck visits on their neighbors. The bear's way of sinking each autumn into the earth to sleep may even have inspired the First Europeans to likewise send their loved ones into the earth at death with the prayer that Bear would guide them to awaken in a fresh otherworld of springtime. It is safe to say that, like other ancient people in the northern half of the world, the First Europeans lived alongside bears and pondered their mysteries, though exactly how those mysteries looked to them is beyond modern knowing.

I also don't know how the listening I practice compares with spiritualities of Indigenous peoples today, either in North America or elsewhere. Listening to nature began for me in the act of feeling affection for other beings—enjoying a birch tree in childhood, finding comfort in the appearance of an eagle during a difficult time as an adult. From Indigenous writers and philosophers, I continue to learn much about Earth-worthy values, and a decade of ceremonies with an Ojibwa-trained medicine man helped me open again as an adult to prayer and faith. Many people in many parts of the world have developed their own ways of listening to nature, and the wisdom gleaned by all such careful listeners is exactly the wisdom needed in today's world. The way of listening I portray here is not intended to imitate the ways of any other people but rather, in parallel with them, to inquire with a sincere heart into what is real.

People sometimes ask, "Is talking with Bear like channeling?" I can't say, since I have never attended a channeling session. I still appreciate Bear's response to this question: "It is good to be wary of the term *channeling* because it communicates a feeling of separation and distance between the everyday and the Helper's calm, abiding voice." What people need instead is to feel the closeness of spirit to their own hearts, the unfailing love and support available to them directly, no proxy needed, in every moment of life.

I often wonder why people don't ask, "Is talking with a Helper like praying?" My own avenues to this path were prayer and meditation, and I'm quicker to see similarities there. When I was a child, the adults who taught me to pray believed in opening the heart and becoming aware of God's love, and it seems to me that there is no better place to start. However, when I followed those suggestions in earlier parts of my life, I never could hear any clear replies. Perhaps the God I was praying to was just too far away, or perhaps I didn't yet trust my own perception strongly enough to hear answers when they arrived. But I can imagine that those who taught me to pray might be overjoyed, as I was, to find a form of prayer where one does not address a huge and empty sky but rather hears spirit speaking back, though in considering this path they would likely have their own mental hurdles to overcome, as I did.

When people who are trying to understand this path jump to "channeling" rather than "prayer" or "meditation," I hear something else: that this path of talking with an unseen Helper is foreign, occult, outside the mainstream. Prayer and meditation are what people in "world" religions do, while talking with a Helper belongs to Indigenous traditions or esoteric paths.

It reminds me, with a pang, that *none* of the four religions followed by more than 75 percent of the world's people (Christianity, Islam, Hinduism, and Buddhism) focuses first and foremost on humans' relatedness with the more-than-human world—with the matrix or family-community in which we are but newcomers. None of them studies the wisdom that billions of organisms have been patiently developing over millions of years or teaches, as a first duty, the human responsibility to live peaceably and respectfully with our more-than-human kin. Though each of them may have the potential to do so, none of them originated by bringing people to center through helping them find their place in the natural world—in the "land of spirit."

It also sends a poignant reminder that books and classes on "world" religions often do not include nature-based faiths, whether Indigenous or Pagan or other, despite the fact that an estimated 6 percent of the world's people follow Indigenous traditions alone. (Indigenous religions are placed instead in anthropology.) While some universities today include programs in religion *and* nature, I know of no programs in religion *of* nature, even though environmental philosophy and environmental ethics have been mainstream for some time. This is yet more evidence of the spirit-matter split in Western thinking, a split that will need to be addressed from many different directions if we have any hope of healing the environmental crises that face us today: climate change, species extinctions, and economic inequality—interlocking symptoms of the same illness, namely, *using* the Earth and its creatures more than *loving* them.

The malady—using more than loving—suggests its own remedy: More loving. More relationship. More regard for the welfare of other creatures, whether human or more-than-human. This path is not about talking with animals, though it might include that; it is not about engaging in shamanic Journeys, though it might include that as well. *This path is about rearranging life to honor interconnection.* Recognizing the indwelling spirit, the fresh-springing currents, in every form of life, human and other. Making room—and time—in every arena of living, from individual experience to social and economic life, for considering the welfare of others. Because only by accommodating ourselves in this way to relationship will we be able to make Earth-worthy decisions—choices that promote the web of life rather than undermine it.

Acknowledgments

The conversations in this book are taken from my transcriptions of Journeys with Bear between March 2013 and New Year's Day 2014, with additions in the Afterword from 2015 and 2016. Occasionally I interpolated a quote from a later conversation, usually indicating the time difference in the text. Sometimes I melded together several conversations taking place in the same few-week period. Both Bear's words and mine have been lightly edited.

I am grateful to Chris D. for introducing me to Bear and providing a model of impeccable listening. Thank you to Mimi Kusch for seeing this book years before I did. I am grateful to Ananya Vajpeyi for permission to reprint her translation of the beautiful lines from her father's poem that open this book.

For his unending love and support, I am grateful to Tim, who laughs at Bear's jokes and who gets me better than anyone else. Except, of course, for Bear.

Thank you, Bear, for being my Helper and Friend.

PRISCILLA STUCKEY is a writer and spiritual counselor with a passion for reconnecting people with nature, including their own natures. Her first book, *Kissed by a Fox: And Other Stories of Friendship in Nature*, won the 2013 WILLA Award in Creative Nonfiction. Priscilla received a PhD from the Graduate Theological Union in Berkeley, CA, in religious studies and feminist theory. She has taught humanities and writing in the graduate programs of Prescott College, and Naropa University. A longtime book editor and writing coach, Stuckey has worked with major publishing houses and writers in North America and abroad. In Oakland she founded an urban creek–based land trust and led creek cleanups and restoration projects. In Boulder she cofounded a local rights-of-nature group. She lives at the base of the Sandia Mountains near Albuquerque with her partner, Tim, and their dog, Bodhi.